Yarn Whirled

Fairy Tales, Fables and Folklore

Pat Olski

Characters You Can Craft With Yarn

DOVER PUBLICATIONS, INC.

Mineola, New York

Dedication

Dedicated with love to Rich, RJ, and Connor

Acknowledgment

I would like to acknowledge, with gratitude, my intrepid editor, Vanessa Putt, who was willing to take a chance on my vision, based on nothing more than a homely, hastily cobbled together sample.

Photography Credits:

Nick Barese: cover and group shots
Cynthia Castellari: individual shots and step-by-step photography

Bibliographical Note

Yarn Whirled™: Fairy Tales, Fables and Folklore is a new work, first published by Dover Publications, Inc., in 2016.

Library of Congress Cataloging-in-Publication Data

Names: Olski, Pat, author.
Title: Yarn whirled : fairy tales, fables and folklore : characters you can
   craft with yarn / Pat Olski.
Description: Mineola, New York : Dover Publications, 2016.
Identifiers: LCCN 2016038930| ISBN 9780486810812 (paperback) | ISBN
   048681081X
Subjects: LCSH: Soft toy making—Patterns. | Yarn. | BISAC: CRAFTS &
HOBBIES
   / Toymaking. | CRAFTS & HOBBIES / Stuffed Animals.
Classification: LCC TT174.3 .O47 2016 | DDC 745.592—dc23 LC record
available at https://lccn.loc.gov/2016038930

Manufactured in the United States by LSC Communications
81081X01   2016
www.doverpublications.com

Yarn Whirled

Fairy Tales, Fables and Folklore

CONTENTS

THE PROJECTS

THE SNOW WHITE COLLECTION

THE NUTCRACKER COLLECTION

THE HANSEL AND GRETEL COLLECTION

THE CINDERELLA COLLECTION

Introduction

Yes, you can!

Otherwise known as the ABCs of making adorable yarn characters . . .

All you need is yarn!

Beginners welcome!

Choosing a character is the hardest part!

When I was about four years old, my favorite craft was to make knitted doll clothing on a knitting spool—for the uninitiated, that's a thread spool with four nails at the top. I always (or in my mind, at least) had the patience to hook the yarn over the nails to make the knitted tube. My mother would bind off the top edge, wet the tube, and then she would place a pencil judiciously into the irregular fabric to form armholes. But the hours I spent waiting for the wet dress to dry were interminable. Even then, I was enticed to create with yarn, but I wanted instant results.

Pre-internet, I was continually on an elusive quest to find quick and appealing yarn-craft patterns that suited my evolving skill levels. In my teens, as a novice knitter, sweaters seemed to be out of my league in terms of skill, time, and expense. Undaunted, I thought, "I'll make mittens!" But, I had barely mastered knitting with two needles, and the only mitten patterns I could find required four—or worse yet, five needles. The lure of the yarn was strong, but the right projects remained inaccessible.

Over time, my skill level and patience increased. However, I still like to enjoy a simple project in between some of my more complicated endeavors. Ironically, browsing and selecting from the seemingly endless array of online patterns now can easily pose the greatest threat to my time!

My *Yarn Whirled* characters can be made in a day. I think that these scrumptious figures are the perfect way to indulge your yarn cravings, with little knowledge, and little time required!

All you need is yarn!

Really, truly. Everyone who picks up these figures is amazed at the structure and flexibility they possess. The figures are made out of nothing but yarn. There is no armature, no wire foundation, nothing but yarn. There are physical forces at

work that transform soft, floppy pieces of yarn into a firm sculpture. Initially I had thought it might be a result of the properties inherent in synthetic yarn, but I have had similar results with wool and cotton. I am sure that it is a product of the force from the twisting of the yarn with the subsequent wrapping of the yarn, but I am not a physicist. To me, it is simply magical!

Beginners Welcome!

I know this seems unbelievable, but it is really true. No prior knowledge and no yarn-craft skills are needed, other than the ability to follow directions, to wrap yarn, and to tie a simple knot. Just wrap the yarn smoothly and firmly, and you will have a delightful figure in very little time.

Choosing a character is the hardest part!

Most of the figures in this book follow the same basic directions for a large doll. They are all equally suited for a beginner. The other figures are no more difficult, but do not follow the same directions. The Celtic princess, Trembling, and the African princess, Chinye, are among the simplest designs in the book.

From Yarn to "Yarn Whirled"

Yarn is irresistible. It has it <u>all</u>—exquisite color, appealing texture, and most importantly, unlimited potential. It represents calm and creativity, productivity and relaxation. It is so enticing. Few people can walk by a skein of yarn on a table without wanting to touch it.

Inextricably tangled in its lure, I have used yarn to knit, crochet, embroider, needlepoint, knot rugs, felt, tat, macramé, weave, make pom-poms and tassels, braids and temari balls, fringe, and cording. I experimented with some techniques, became expert at others. I was pretty confident that I had exhausted all of the possibilities in this medium. I have been very fortunate to have been able to have a career in the yarn industry, teaching and designing.

I thought I had sampled all of the applications, and that all that was left was for me to deepen my skill level, until . . .

As random as novel ideas often are, I was struck with the idea of making a yarn doll for a class that I was teaching to young elementary-school students. An exhaustive internet search did not unearth anything similar to what I had in mind. I decided to design my own doll.

In retrospect, this idea was actually a confluence of past memories, projects, and techniques. I have a fond recollection of a hand-crocheted hat made by my mother for me when I was six, which I only wanted to wear because it had simple tassels that were knotted to look like dolls at the end of the ties. As a child, I made dolls out of yarn, felt, clay, fabric, and beads. I had a decided mental image of what I wanted those dolls to look like, and rarely was I satisfied. When my friends started to have babies, I made a number of cloth dolls to give away. Later, as the mother of two boys, my doll-making career came to an abrupt end! As a designer, I have been asked to knit and crochet yarn toys for publication, and I have thoroughly enjoyed the experience—but until now, none of them were dolls.

When I first experimented with the yarn doll, my intent was to make nothing fancier than a glorified tassel with braided limbs—an idea that goes back to the pioneer corn-husk and straw dolls. But, as I worked on my first doll, I was amazed at how firm the yarn was when wrapped together, and I was surprised with the results. Different iterations yielded better and better outcomes. I couldn't believe how seamlessly the whole idea came together. When I disliked the original idea I had for a shoe, a quick trial with wrapping each side of the foot separately yielded a flexible, perfectly proportionate, foot, in a manner I couldn't have planned for if I had tried. The original dolls I created had a simple tie at each end of a bundle to create a hand. When I saw the strands of yarn lying smoothly on the board, the idea popped into my mind to try making a thumb. I thought the yarn would be too bulky and the thumb too fiddly, but yet again, I was pleasantly surprised.

The dolls in this book represent the forward progression of my techniques. I can only say that despite all of my planning and experience, it was the properties of the yarn itself that ultimately dictated the proportions and designs of these adorable characters, and that is really how "Yarn Whirled" was created.

Materials and Tips

Scissors

Sturdy, sharp scissors are a must to cut through the layers of yarn. Dull scissors will fray the edges of the yarn.

Needles

A blunt, smooth tapestry needle with an eye large enough for your yarn is a necessity. I keep an assortment of needles from size 13–16 on a magnet at my work space, so I have a place to park my needles while I work. I prefer metal needles.

But, why do I need a needle if I don't need to know how to sew to make these characters? Great question. The needle is used to bury the ends of yarn into the doll and to affix the hair to the head. You can knot the hair piece to the head and use a crochet hook to pull the yarn ends into an inconspicuous place. However, a needle can do those things and more, and you will find it easier to use than the methods that I have just mentioned.

If you wish to stitch on the features, a needle is necessary. Nevertheless, there are many non-stitching facial-feature options for the truly needle-averse. You may paint, glue, or snap on the eyes, nose, and mouth. Craft stores are full of no-sew options for doll makers.

Rulers and tape measures

A good straight edge ruler is needed to measure and mark the center points on your board. A tape measure is necessary to measure the circumference of an object, such as the ball of yarn used to fill the head.

Marker pens and powder blush

I use a very fine-tipped, permanent, acid-free marker to gently sketch on the eyebrows. Lightly "dotting" with the marker tip is more effective than trying to draw a straight line across strands of yarn. I use my fingertip to smooth on powder blush in a circle on the cheeks. It is remarkably long-lasting, and the powder covers the unevenness of the yarn.

Choosing a board

You will need a board made of cardboard, wood, or plastic to wrap the yarn around. Pieces of mat board or corrugated cardboard glued together work well. The dimensions are stated with each pattern. Just be certain that the board has smooth edges so that the yarn will not snag and that the board is sturdy enough so it does not bend, buckle, or snap from the pressure of the wrapped yarn. Use a permanent marker to mark the center point of each edge.

Yarn

To my surprise and delight, I have had success with all types of yarn, from synthetics to natural fiber. When you select yarn for the body of the doll, choose a yarn that is strong enough to be wrapped with a certain degree of tension. I believe that the firmness and evenness of the resulting wraps is more important than the composition of the fiber. When using wool, my preference is to use superwash treated wool for the body, because it has a slightly smoother appearance than untreated wool. Test the yarn for strength and appearance by wrapping it around your fingers. Some yarns form lovely smooth wraps, and some look rather rope-y. Depending upon your yarn choices and your own yarn wrap tension, you may need to make fewer or additional wraps to have complete coverage. As a rule of thumb, each large doll that is wrapped completely in the body color (as is the Princess in Gold) takes about 180–200yds/165m–183m of a DK–worsted weight yarn in the body/head color to complete.

This is the perfect craft to make use of novelty yarns with unusual texture and fiber. Every fiber from silk to raffia has a unique appearance and can only enhance your finished character. Trendy ruffle, net, and fabric yarns are perfect for quick coverage and unusual effects. The only caveat would be to save the more fragile yarns for the clothing and embellishments.

Key Points for Success

* Do not wrap your yarn too tightly. You do not want the board to buckle, bend, or break. With practice you should be able to make smooth, even wraps.

* Remember, as crazy as this seems, you may be building muscles in your hands you are not used to using. With time, the wrapping and twisting will not be tiring.

* The "order of operations" that I have detailed in the basic directions is the one that worked best for me. It is easiest to wrap the shoes and legs before making the head.

* You will be surprised at how little the yarn "unwinds" while you are working with it. However, if you are concerned, you may always tape down loose ends while you have pieces set aside—for instance, the thumbs—until you pick them up to work on them again.

* Save your yarn scraps. They are perfect to use to fill the center of the yarn ball that is used to stuff the head.

* Threading a thick yarn into a tapestry needle can be a feat. So, I suggest wrapping the yarn around the eye of the needle, pinching the bend firmly, and then trying to thread the bend through the eye. It takes some practice, but it really works. If you are working with a novelty yarn, you may wish to fold a tiny piece of paper over the end of the yarn and then insert the paper-covered yarn end into the needle.

* If you want to smooth the yarn used for a fringed hair piece or skirt, iron it! I iron the fringe, combed out carefully, following the manufacturer's directions for the yarn, and I use a press cloth over the yarn to be safe. Remember, you want to smooth the yarn, not flatten it entirely!

* After I have embroidered the eyes, I wet the eyelash floss and use the tip of my tapestry needle to fan out the eyelashes. Once they are dry, I trim them.

* Once the doll is finished, I give it a haircut. Because the hair consists of layers of yarn, you may need to move the hair gently and trim the ends a few times until you are satisfied.

Getting Started with Step-by-Step Techniques

Wind yarn around board for
desired number of wraps to
make a bundle.

Constrictor Knot

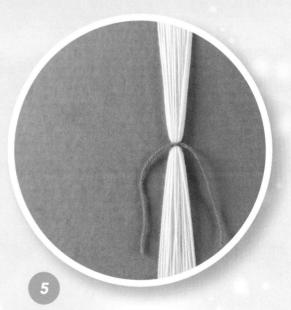

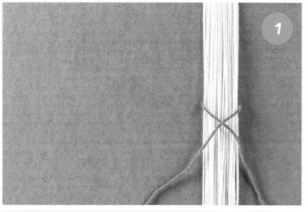

1. Fold yarn piece in half. Place yarn under bundle, with halfway point centered. Bring right and left tails to front. Cross the tails over the front of the bundle, right over left (facing you).

2. Wrap the right tail around the back of the work, under the bundled yarn.

3. Bring to front under the left tail.

4. Bring yarn over the left tail and slide it under the previously made cross.

Finished bundle tied on one side with a constrictor knot.

Lark's Head Knot

 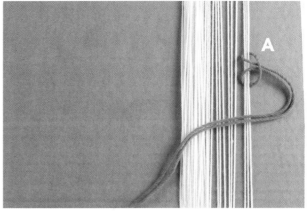

Fold knot yarn(s) in half. Slide loop (A) under the foundation (wrapped) yarn.

Take 2 cut ends of knot yarn, fold them over foundation (wrapped) yarn, and then insert them into loop (A) created at top of bend. Pull gently.

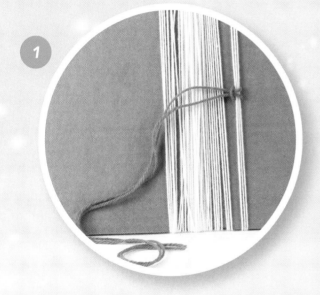

Use a series of Lark's Head Knots to secure a wrapped fringe, as for a wig.

Arm Bundle

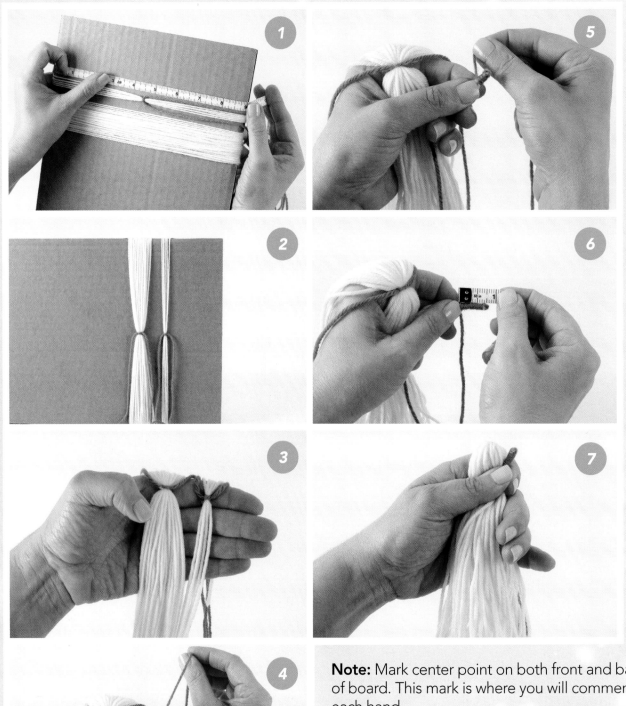

Note: Mark center point on both front and back of board. This mark is where you will commence each hand.

1. Knot at top of doll's thumb.

2. Knot at top of doll's hand.

3. Remove from board.

4–5. Pinch and wrap thumb.

6. Completed thumb.

7. Pinch thumb and hand at wrist.

Arm Bundle

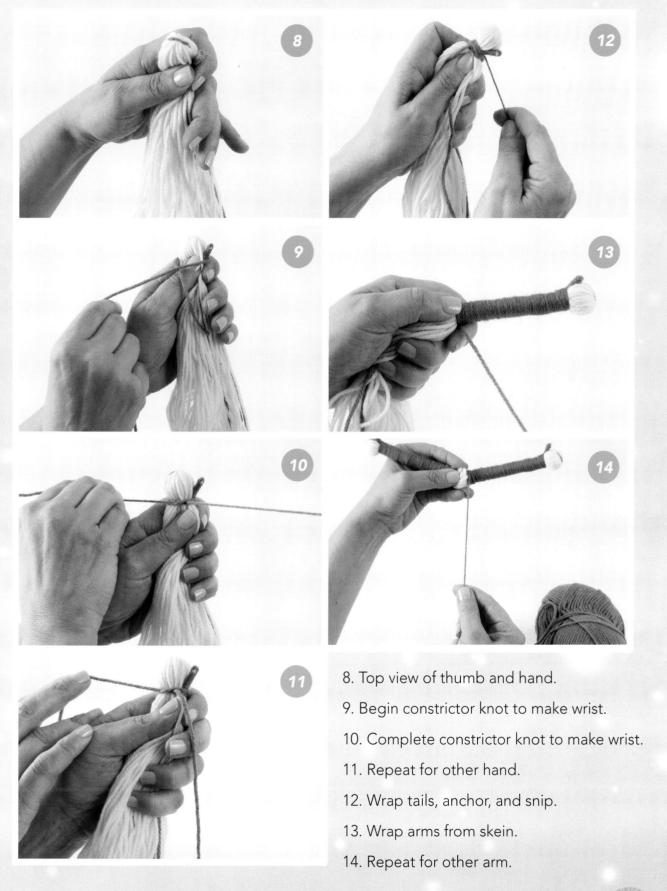

8. Top view of thumb and hand.

9. Begin constrictor knot to make wrist.

10. Complete constrictor knot to make wrist.

11. Repeat for other hand.

12. Wrap tails, anchor, and snip.

13. Wrap arms from skein.

14. Repeat for other arm.

Head * Body * Leg Bundle (Make 2)

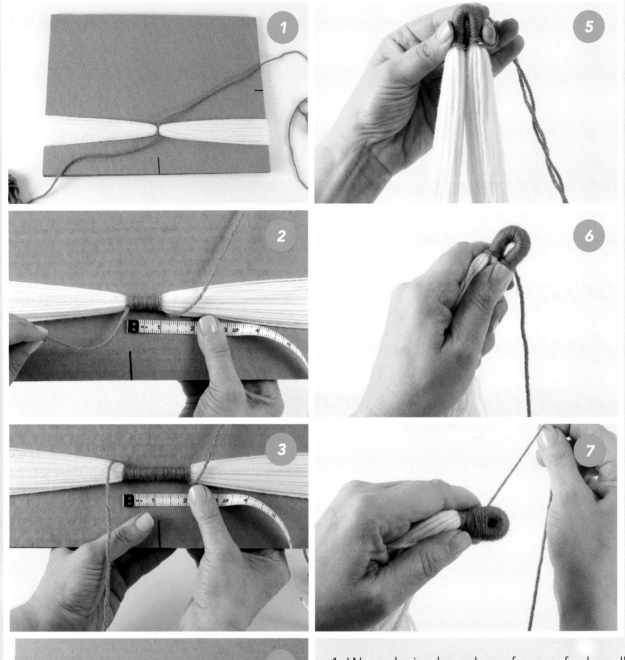

1. Wrap desired number of wraps for bundle, then tie at halfway point with constrictor knot to form center of shoe.

2. Wrap shoe yarn for one inch to right of knot.

3. Wrap shoe yarn for one inch to left of knot.

4. Flip board over. Make a temporary knot for top of head.

5. Remove bundle from board.

6. Bend shoe at center knot.

7. Wrap at bend to secure.

Head * Body * Leg Bundle

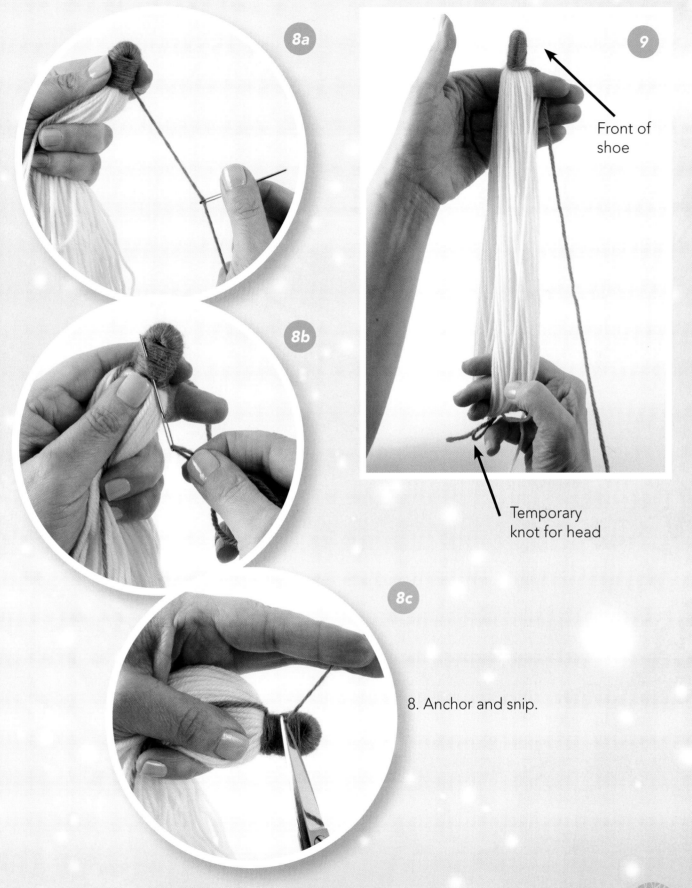

8a

8b

8c

9

Front of shoe

Temporary knot for head

8. Anchor and snip.

Head * Body * Leg Bundle

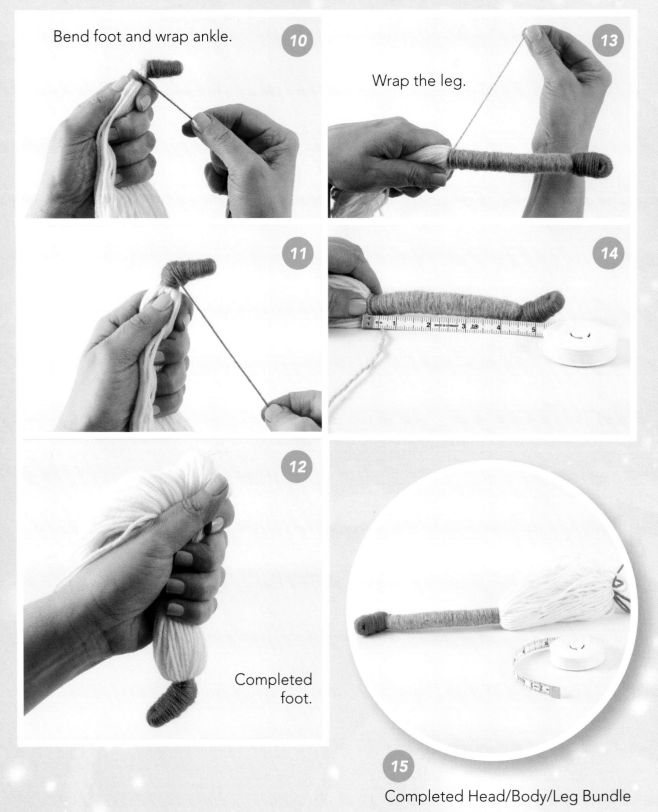

Bend foot and wrap ankle.

10

11

12

Completed
foot.

Wrap the leg.

13

14

15

Completed Head/Body/Leg Bundle

Winding Yarn into a Ball

1

2

3

4

5

6 Measure the diameter of the yarn ball.

Head * Body * Leg Bundle

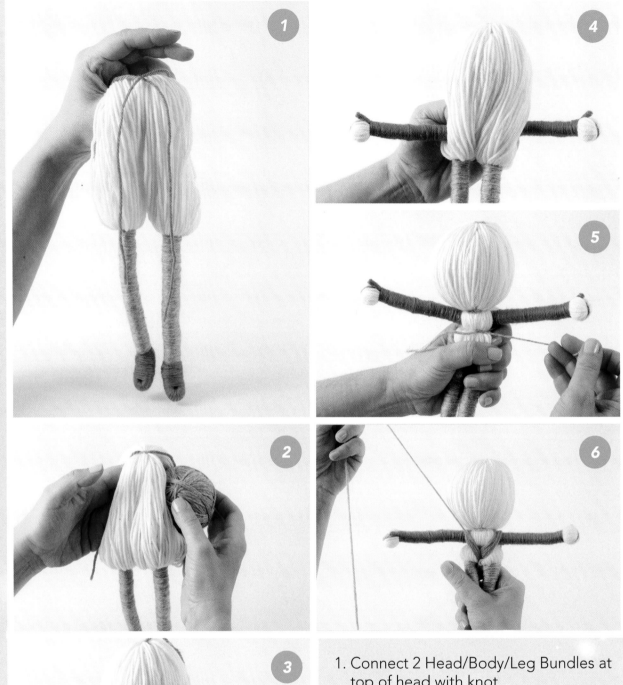

1. Connect 2 Head/Body/Leg Bundles at top of head with knot.
2. Place ball of yarn inside head.
3. Place paper in between front and back to keep separate.
4. Insert arm bundle into body.
5. Tie a piece of yarn with constrictor knot at neck, and knot a piece of yarn under the arms for waist.
6. Attach and wrap shirt yarn from crotch over shoulders.

Head * Body * Leg Bundle

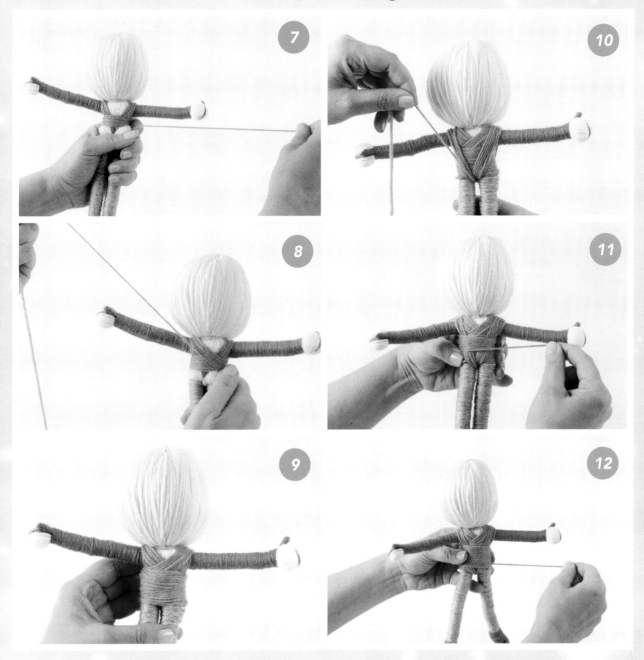

7. Wrap yarn around waist.

8. Wrap yarn from waist over shoulders.

9. Wrap yarn around waist and hips.

10–12. Repeat sequence until body is fully covered.

Hair Fringe

1. Wrap yarn.
2. Secure with Lark's Head Knots.
3. Remove from board, and cut at bottom.
4. Fold fringe in half, using a piece of paper to separate the sides.
5. Sew together at knots, creating a center part.
6. Doll with hair sewn onto head.

Hair Using Lark's Head Knot Method

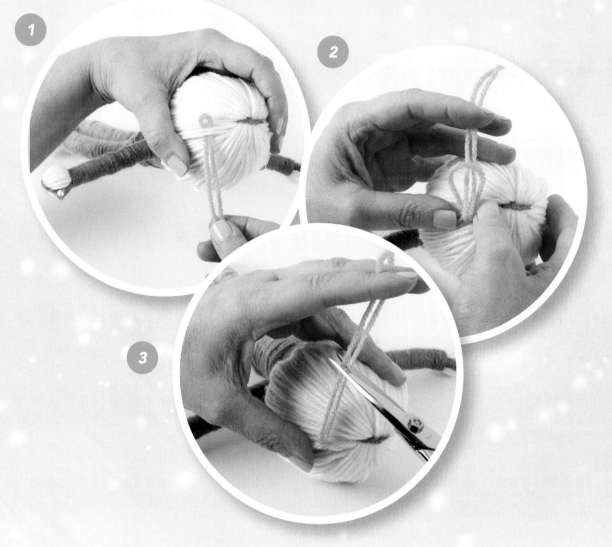

1

2

3

Putting Off Loose Yarn Ends

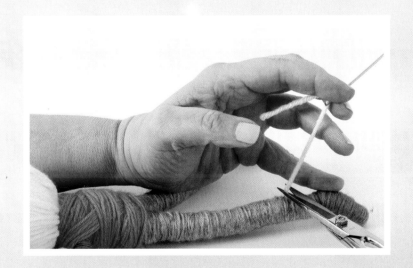

Basic Directions for the Large Doll

FINISHED HEIGHT Approximately 11in/28cm

MATERIALS

All figures require sharp scissors, a ruler, stiff cardboard, and a large, blunt-tipped tapestry needle. A stiff piece of paper is helpful to keep the strands of hair separate. A crochet hook will make it easier to form the knots on dolls with knotted-on hair.

Each pattern will specify the yarn needed.

NOTE

The abbreviation MC is used for the main color in each pattern.

TECHNIQUE GLOSSARY

Anchor and Snip

Anchor all loose yarn ends by threading each end through the tapestry needle and burying it in the center of the bundle. Snip excess.

Yarn Tail

Pieces of yarn on either side of a knot, or a piece of yarn left at the end of a wrap.

Constrictor Knot

Place a piece of yarn under the bundle, with the halfway point of the yarn centered. Bring the right and left tails to the front. Cross the tails over the front of the bundle, right over left. Wrap the right tail around the back of the work, then bring it to the front under the left tail, and then over the left tail and under the previously made cross. Pull both tails slowly until knot is tight enough.

Lark's Head Knot

Fold the yarn piece(s) in half. Slide the loop under the foundation yarn. Take the cut ends of the yarn, fold them over the foundation yarn, and insert them into the loop created at the top of the bend. Pull gently.

NOTE: Wrap the yarn evenly and smoothly, but not too tightly, around the board. You do not want the board to buckle, and you want to be able to remove the yarn bundle easily.

HEAD/BODY/LEG BUNDLE (Make 2)

Wrap the body-color yarn 65 times around a 12in/30.5cm board. Mark a line showing the center of the board. Cut the yarn.

MAKE THE SHOE

* Fold a 120in/305cm piece of shoe-color yarn in half and mark the center. Slide the yarn under the wrapped yarn, lining up the center mark with the middle of the wrapped yarn. Tie a constrictor knot around the wrapped yarn at the center line of the board. There should be two tails each about 59in/150cm long. Wrap one tail around the bundle firmly and evenly for 1in/2.5cm, then wrap from the center line out in the other direction with the second yarn tail for 1in/2.5cm. Carefully remove the bundle from the board. Fold the bundle in half at the constrictor knot tie line, and wrap one yarn tail firmly around the shoe a number of times to secure; anchor the yarn end, and snip. Fold the foot at the ankle; wrap the remaining yarn tail around the ankle, then around the heel until all of the body yarn of the heel is covered. Anchor and snip.

* Use another 12in/30.5cm piece of yarn to loosely tie the other end of the bundle at the exact opposite end from the shoe, which will be for the head. This tie is temporary.

LEGS

* Wrap the legs with yarn directly from the skein[†]. Anchor the end and make a few very tight wraps at the ankle, then wrap up the leg for 4½ in/11.5cm from the ankle and 5in/12.5cm from the bottom of the heel. Anchor and snip. Wrap the other leg to match, <u>making sure that the feet are both facing in the same direction</u>.

† The yarn color will be specified in the pattern. If done in a color other than the body color, this will create leggings or trousers.

HEAD

* Take the two bundles and thread a 12in/30.5cm piece of body yarn through both head pieces. Tie together firmly, using a constrictor knot. Make sure the knot is directly opposite the shoes. Remove the temporary ties.

* Wind a ball of body-color yarn that measures 2.5in/6cm in diameter and 8in/20cm in circumference.

* Place the ball inside the head bundle, smoothing the yarn and centering the ball carefully. Push the ball as high into the head as possible.

* Using a 12in/30.5cm piece of body yarn, firmly tie a constrictor knot for the neck, approximately 2¾in/7cm from the top of the head. Smooth the head, making sure that the ball is centered and that the neck yarn is positioned firmly against the bottom of the yarn ball.

* Place a ruler or folded paper between the bundles to keep the front and back body yarn separate until the arm piece is completed.

ARM BUNDLE

* Wrap body-color yarn 45 times around a 9in/23cm board for the arms. Mark a line showing the center of the board. *At the center (4½ in/5cm) mark, using a 12in/30.5 cm piece of body yarn, make a constrictor knot to tie the five outer strands together for the thumb. Then, with a 12in/30.5cm piece of body-color yarn, firmly tie the remaining 40 strands together at the same point. Flip the board over and repeat from *. Be careful to center each knot so that the arms are the same length. Carefully remove from the board.

* To create the thumb, wrap one yarn tail from the thumb knot tightly around the five strands for about ¾in/2 cm. Pinch the base of the thumb and hand together at the wrist and wrap the other yarn tail firmly and evenly around the thumb joint, then tightly around the wrist.

* Cut an 8in/20.25cm piece of yarn and tie a constrictor knot around the wrist, being careful to hold the thumb in place.

* Working from the skein[†], wrap the yarn firmly and evenly around the arm bundle and knots until you have reached the center. Repeat for the other side, making sure that the thumbs are both on the same side of the hand. Anchor, hide, and snip all threads.

† The yarn color will be specified in the pattern. If done in a color other than the body color, this will create sleeves.

BODY

* Insert the arm piece into the body bundles in the space under the head, being careful to keep the front and back strands separate. Cut an 18in/46cm piece of body yarn, and tie a constrictor knot firmly under the arm bundle, creating a waist. Make sure the arm bundle is centered and pressed firmly under the neck wrap.

* Using yarn from the skein[†], wrap yarn evenly and smoothly eight times from the crotch (between the legs under the waist) to the right shoulder, then eight times from the crotch to the left shoulder. Wrap the yarn twelve times from the waist down to define the hips, covering the previous work evenly. Wrap eight times from the left waist over the right shoulder, then from the right waist over the left shoulder. Wrap the yarn twenty times around the body from the underarm to the hip, covering the previous work evenly. Wrap the yarn evenly and smoothly eight times from the crotch to the right shoulder, then eight times from the crotch to the left shoulder. Wrap the yarn smoothly from the underarm to the hip until the previous work is covered smoothly. Repeat the wraps, if necessary, to cover the body.

† The yarn color will be specified in the pattern. If done in a color other than the body color, this will create a shirt, blouse, or bodice.

* Create the hips by wrapping yarn directly from the skein [†] in a figure-8 pattern. Work *from the front of the right upper hip, around the back of the right hip, between the legs to the left front hip, around the back of the left hip, and between the legs to the front right hip. Repeat from *, building up the yarn in successive wraps, starting at the hips and ending at the upper thigh, until the hip area is neatly covered and the shape is pleasing. Anchor and snip.

† The yarn color will be specified in the pattern. If done in a color other than the body color, this will create bloomers.

HAIR

* Wrap the hair yarn 120 times around a 9in/23cm board. Cut yarn. Fold a 40in/102cm piece of hair yarn in half and secure the first bundle of twelve strands with a lark's head knot at the center point of the board. Continue to tie fringe by using a series of lark's head knots across the wraps, making ten bunches of twelve strands each. Cut the fringe open opposite the secured edge. Remove from the board. Fold the hair piece in half using a piece of paper to keep the fringe separate. Thread a tapestry needle with hair yarn and sew the center knots together, lacing from one to the next to close the center seam. Place the wig on the head and sew on or knot on to secure.

FACE

* If the pattern indicates an eye color, the eye is embroidered in the manner of the eye diagram chart (see page 26). Use six strands of black floss for the pupil and lashes, six strands of colored floss for the iris, and six strands of white floss for the highlight of the pupil.

* If the pattern indicates a knot for an eye, then thread a tapestry needle with four six-strand pieces of black embroidery floss; make a French knot for each eye. Lashes are made with a doubled three-strand piece of embroidery floss, knotted on the eye knot. Clip to about ½in/1.25cm. Dampen the floss and comb the strands with the tip of a needle to separate the lashes. Use a single strand of white embroidery floss doubled, then knotted on, or stitched in a small straight stitch for the eye accent.

* Thread a tapestry needle with one six-strand piece of rose embroidery floss to make small straight stitches or knots for the mouth.

* Thread a tapestry needle with a piece of body yarn. Anchor the yarn at one side of the head, and wrap it three times around three strands of the head to make an ear. Bring the needle up at the center front of the face and make a stitch around the center three strands for the nose. Bring the needle up at the other side of the face and wrap it three times around three strands to make the other ear. Anchor and snip.

* Rub blush on cheeks and gently draw Pigma® marker brown eyebrows.

* After stitching or knotting on features, anchor and snip all loose ends of floss to secure and hide.

DIAGRAM FOR LEFT EYE

(Reverse shaping for right eye.)

Knot for eyelashes

Floss tails from knot for eyelashes

Split stitch iris

Direction under facial yarn from straight stitch 1 to 2.

Direction under facial yarn from straight stitch 2 to 3.

Direction under facial yarn from straight stitch 3 to starting point (A) for lazy daisy stitch.

Direction under facial yarn from ending point (C) of lazy daisy stitch, to where floss is brought to front of work to create eyelash knot.

Lazy Daisy Stitch: Commence at starting point (A), and work in a counterclockwise direction. Anchor Lazy Daisy Stitch over one strand of facial yarn at the inner corner of the eye (B), and end the stitch by sliding the needle under the facial yarn, and then exit the needle at the edge of the three black pupil stitches (C).

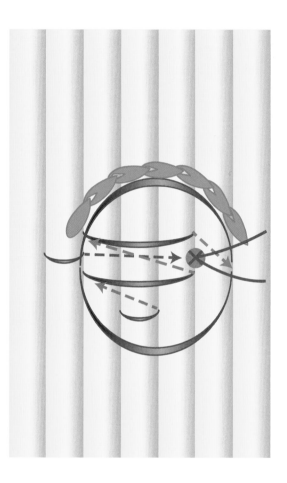

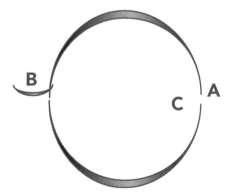

TIPS

* Use yarn that is unwound from the outside of the skein for the head and body, because it will yield smoother pieces of yarn.

* Use the constrictor knot to make a tight knot.

* Note that differing weights of yarn will change the proportions of the finished doll. Thus, a doll made from a DK weight yarn will be more slender than a doll made from a heavy worsted-weight yarn.

* Make sure the back of the doll is covered as evenly as the front.

* Use the eye of a large tapestry needle to smooth the strands into place.

* Economize by using scrap yarn inside the ball of yarn for the head filling.

* Hide all loose ends under wraps as you work.

* When wrapping the legs, give a tight twist every few wraps to firm the legs.

* Be sure to build up the bloomers or top of the legs to keep the skirts from sliding down.

* If a yarn is not strong enough to wrap tightly, wrap the figure with a stronger yarn, and then put a layer of the more fragile yarn on top.

* Hair and fringe skirts may need to be pressed to make them smooth. Steam lightly, following the yarn manufacturer's instructions. You may want to use a press cloth to cover the yarn when you iron.

* To thread a tapestry needle with yarn, fold the yarn in half and pinch the bend firmly. Push the bend through the eye of the needle.

* Wrapped yarn doesn't unwind easily, so pieces such as thumbs can be left unsecured until necessary, without knotting or anchoring the bottoms.

* Facial features can be embroidered, painted, or attached as desired.

Snow White

From "Snow White and Rose Red" by the Brothers Grimm

FINISHED HEIGHT 11½in/29 cm

MATERIALS

Yarn

* Cascade Yarns® 220 Superwash® 3.5oz/100g, 220yds/200m (100% superwash wool)—one skein each: #817 Aran (MC), #900 Charcoal (A), #1946 Silver Grey (B), #1914 Alaska Sky (C), #871 White (D)

* Cascade Yarns® 220 Superwash® Sport 1.75oz/50g, 136yds/125m (100% superwash merino wool)—one skein each: #820 Lemon (E), #1915 Banana Cream (F)

* Small amount of green yarn

Other Tools

* Sharp scissors, a ruler, stiff cardboard, and a large, blunt-tipped tapestry needle

* Six-strand embroidery floss in black, white, light gray-blue, and rose pink

* Powder blush or paint for cheeks

* Pigma #01 micron marker in brown

DOLL

Follow the basic directions for the Large Doll using MC. Do not wrap the legs with MC.

Shoes and Tights: Use A; make the shoes following the basic directions. Starting at the ankles, wrap legs with B to make tights.

Blouse/Bloomers: Use C; follow basic directions. Wrap yarn from shoulder, covering arm completely for about 1in/2.5cm to create the sleeve. Repeat for other sleeve.

Skirt: Cut 22 pieces of D and 44 pieces of C, each 18in/46cm long. Cut a 24in/61cm piece of C and fold it in half. Anchor it to a board and use it as a foundation for a lark's head knot fringe. Each knot is worked with two strands of yarn in a sequence of two knots of C, then one knot of D, repeated

11 times. Trim the fringe to 4in/10cm. Tie the skirt around the waist. Wrap green yarn around waist for the sash.

Hair: Follow basic directions, using one strand each of E and F held together and wrapped 72 times around a 9in/23cm board.

Headband: Cut six 18in/46cm pieces of C. Make a braid using three two-strand pieces. Tie the braid around the hair for the headband. Trim excess yarn.

Face: Follow the basic directions for the Large Doll, using light gray-blue floss to embroider the colored part of the eye.

Rose Red

From "Snow White and Rose Red" by the Brothers Grimm

FINISHED HEIGHT 11in/28cm

MATERIALS

Yarn

* Cascade Yarns® 220 Superwash®
3.5oz/100g, 220yds/200m (100% superwash wool)—one skein each: #817 Aran (MC), #893 Ruby (A), #809 Really Red (B), #1946 Silver Grey (C)

* Cascade Yarns® 220 Superwash® Sport 1.75oz/50g, 136yds/125m (100% superwash merino wool)—one skein each: #818 Mocha (D)

* Small amount of green yarn

Other Tools

* Sharp scissors, a ruler, stiff cardboard, and a large, blunt-tipped tapestry needle

* Six-strand embroidery floss in black, white, light gray blue, and rose pink

* Powder blush or paint for cheeks

* Pigma #01 micron marker in brown

DOLL

Follow the basic directions for the Large Doll using MC. Do not wrap the legs with MC.

Shoes and Tights: Use A; make the shoes following the basic directions. Starting at the ankles, wrap legs with C to make tights.

Blouse/Bloomers: Use A; follow basic directions. Wrap yarn from shoulder, covering arm completely for about 1in/2.5cm to create the sleeve. Repeat for other sleeve.

Skirt: Cut 22 pieces of A and 44 pieces of B, each 18in/46cm long. Cut a 24in/61cm piece of B and fold it in half. Anchor it to a board and use it as a foundation for a lark's head knot fringe. Each knot is worked with two strands of yarn in a sequence of two knots of B, then one knot of A, repeated 11 times. Trim the fringe to 4in/10cm. Tie the skirt around the waist. Wrap green yarn around waist for the sash.

Hair: Use D wrapped 140 times around a 9in/23cm board.

Headband: Cut six 18in/46cm pieces of A. Make a braid using three two-strand pieces. Tie the braid around the hair for the headband. Trim excess yarn.

Face: Follow the basic directions for the Large Doll, using light gray-blue floss to embroider the colored part of the eye.

Bear

From "Snow White and Rose Red" by the Brothers Grimm

FINISHED HEIGHT 9in/23cm

MATERIALS

Yarn

* Cascade Yarns® Pluscious 3.5oz/100g, 148.7yds/136m (100% polyester)—one each: #23 Kangaroo (MC)

* Cascade Yarns® Elysian 3.5oz/100g, 219yds/200m (60% superwash merino wool, 40% acrylic)—one skein each: #19 Tannin (A)

* Small amounts of scrap yarn in similar shade of brown to fill the head and body

* Small amount of red yarn for scarf

Other Tools

* Sharp scissors, a ruler, stiff cardboard, and a large, blunt-tipped tapestry needle

* Six-strand embroidery floss in black and white

DOLL

Follow the basic directions for the Large Doll.

Head/Body/Leg Bundle (Make 2): Wrap MC 85 times around a 9in/23cm board.

Feet and Legs: Using A, wrap the foot for 2½in/6cm for three layers, until the fur from the bundle is fully covered. Bend and wrap the foot and ankle with MC, then wrap the yarn around the leg until leg measures 3½/9cm in circumference and 2½/6cm in length from the ankle bend. Repeat for the other leg.

Head

Earpiece (Make 1): Wrap MC 50 times around a 5in/12.5cm board. Cut a 72in/183cm piece of MC. Fold the yarn in half and make a constrictor knot at one end of the bundle. Wrap the yarn for 2in/5cm from each side of the knot, as if to make shoes. Repeat at other end of bundle. Bend and secure at the midpoints of the bundle for the ears. Place the ear bundle inside the head bundle, centering carefully, with the ears extending outside the bundle.

For the head, wrap a ball of scrap yarn that is 8in/20cm in circumference. Place this ball inside the bundle under the ear bundle.

Cut a 24in/61cm piece of MC. Make a constrictor knot under the head and push it up until it is as close as possible to the bottom of the yarn ball. Wrap the excess yarn around the bundle to create the neck.

Arms: Wrap MC 65 times around a 7in/18cm board. Tie at each end for the paws using cut pieces of MC, 8in/20cm long. Do not make thumbs. Wrap the arms from wrist to wrist, until the upper arm is 3in/7.5cm in circumference. Insert the arm bundle into the body. Tie a 24in/61cm piece of MC around the body directly under the arms to secure the arm bundle.

Body: Wrap scrap yarn into a ball about 6in/15cm in circumference. Place inside the body. *Wrap MC in a V-pattern from shoulder to crotch eight times around each shoulder, then wrap yarn 20 times around the torso from the underarms to the hips. Repeat from * two times, then wrap the yarn in a figure-8 pattern around one hip and leg to the other, wrapping 18 times around each leg. Continue to wrap in this fashion, until the body has a pleasing shape.

Scarf: Cut nine 12in/30.5cm pieces of red yarn, and make a three-strand braid, using three pieces of yarn in each strand. Knot both ends of the scarf, then trim. Tie the scarf around the bear's neck.

Face: Make French-knot eyes from four pieces of six-strand black floss, and stitch a straight-stitch nose. Embroider a straight-stitch eye accent using four strands of white floss.

FINISHED HEIGHT 11in/28cm

MATERIALS

Yarn

* Red Heart® Super Saver™ 7oz/198g, 364yds/333m (100% acrylic)—one skein each: #E300-316 Soft White (MC), #E300-0505 Aruba Sea (A), #E300-235 Lemon (B), #300-320 Cornmeal (C)

* Red Heart® Boutique Unforgettable™ 3.5oz/100g, 280yds/256m (100% acrylic)—one skein each: #E793-3960 Tidal (D)

* Red Heart® Boutique Swanky™ 3.5oz/100g, 202yds/185m (62% acrylic, 38% polyester)—one skein each: #E819-9522 Teal Essence (E)

* Red Heart Boutique Sashay Metallic™ 3.5oz/100g, 30yds/27m (66% acrylic, 23% polyester, 11% metallic)—one skein each: #E782M-9944 Malachite (F)

* Red Heart® Super Saver™ Accent™ 4oz/113g, 202yds/184m (100% acrylic)—small amount: E303-625 Guava (G)

Other Tools

* Sharp scissors, a ruler, stiff cardboard, and a large, blunt-tipped tapestry needle

* Six-strand embroidery floss in black, light orchid purple, lime green, black, white, and rose pink

* Powder blush or paint for cheeks

* Pigma #01 micron marker in brown

* Two green pipe cleaners for wings

* A pencil for wrapping the flowers

Doll

Follow the basic directions for the Large Doll, using MC for the body.

Hair: Follow the basic directions for the Large Doll, using one strand each of B and C held together and wrapped 60 times.

Shoes and Bloomers: Use A.

Bodice: Use D.

Belt: Wrap E four or five times over the waist. Anchor and snip.

Skirt: Cut ten 12in/30.5cm pieces of F. Fold the pieces over the belt, and trim to desired length. Wrap additional yarn in E over waistband to secure.

Face: Follow the basic directions for the Large Doll. Eyes are made with four-strand black French knots. Eyelashes are an anchored and knotted doubled six-strand piece of black floss. Eye accent is a straight stitch made of four strands of white floss.

Accessories

Floral Wreath: Fold 48in/122cm piece of E in half. Twist yarn tightly until it doubles back on itself. Fold it in half, and let it coil into a rope. Knot ends to make a circle for the wreath. Trim with five embroidery-floss flowers.

Floss Flowers (make 5): Tape 12in/30.5cm piece of green floss along a pencil. Wrap purple floss over the pencil six times. Clip ends and tie the green floss in a knot to make the flower. Knot flower onto wreath with green floss. Clip green ends to same size as purple fringes. Trim flower. If you trim the floss when it is damp it is easier to trim and fluff with the blunt tip of a needle.

Wings: Fold two pipe cleaners into the shape of wings. Drape F over wings, wrapping around pipe cleaners occasionally to secure. Sew or knot the wings onto the body, catching a few pieces of the yarn to secure further.

Clara

Adapted from The Nutcracker and the Mouse King by E. T. A. Hoffmann

FINISHED HEIGHT 12in/30.5cm

MATERIALS

Yarn

* Premier® Yarns Deborah Norville Collection™ Everyday® Soft Worsted 4oz/113g, 203yds/186m (100% anti-pilling acrylic)—one skein each: #ED100-02 Cream (MC), #ED100-06 Baby Pink (A), #100-01 Snow White (B), and #100-11 Chocolate (C)

Other Tools

* Sharp scissors, a ruler, stiff cardboard, and a large, blunt-tipped tapestry needle

* Six-strand embroidery floss in black, white, green, and rose pink

* Powder blush or paint for cheeks

* Pigma #01 micron marker in brown

DOLL

Follow the basic directions for the Large Doll using MC.

Shoes: Use A to make the shoes. Once the legs have been wrapped with MC, fold an 18in/46cm piece of A in half, and, at the halfway mark, knot it to the back of the shoe. Crisscross the ends of yarn around the leg, and tie in the back to create a ballet slipper. Repeat for the other shoe.

Bodice/Bloomers: Use A. Add a few additional wraps on each side to drape over the shoulders.

Tutu: Wrap one strand each of A and B held together 100 times around a 5in/12.5cm board. Use a 36in/91cm piece of A to create a fringe (see the basic directions for the hair), making 20 bunches of ten strands each. Trim the fringe to 3in/7.5cm. Wrap this fringe around the doll's waist twice, and knot to secure. Wrap A around the waist to hide the knots and to secure the fringe. Anchor and snip.

Face: Follow the basic directions for the Large Doll, using green floss to embroider the colored part of the eye.

Hair: Follow the basic directions for the Large Doll. Use C, wrapped 120 times around a 9in/23cm board. Once the hair is attached to the doll's head, trim a few front pieces to create bangs. Tease the yarn with the tip of a tapestry needle to separate the fibers. Cut three 12in/30.5cm pieces of A, and tie them around a few pieces of hair in a bow. Trim the ends.

Nutcracker

Adapted from The Nutcracker and the Mouse King by E. T. A. Hoffmann

FINISHED HEIGHT 8in/20cm

MATERIALS

Yarn

* Cascade Yarns® Elysian 3.5oz/100g, 219yds/200m (60% superwash merino wool, 40% acrylic)—one skein each: #19 Tannin (MC), #03 Pirate Black (A), #15 Nautical Blue (B), #38 Pale Marigold (C), #01 White (D)

* Cascade Yarns® Pluscious 3.5oz/100g, 148.7yds/136m (100% polyester)—one skein each: #19 Caviar (E)

* Cascade Yarns® 220 Superwash® 3.5oz/100g, 220yds/200m (100% superwash wool)—one skein each: #809 Really Red (F)

* Small amount of gray yarn

Other Tools

* Same as for Nutcracker Prince (Green embroidery floss not needed.)

DOLL

Follow the basic directions for the Large Doll. Wrap MC 65 times around a 9in/23cm board for each head/body bundle. Make 1½in/4cm ball of yarn to stuff the head. Use a constrictor knot to tie the two bundles together at the top using a 72in/183cm piece of E. Place a piece of paper between the front and back of each bundle to keep them separate. Tie a 12in/30.5cm piece of MC 3in/7.5cm from the top of the bundle for the neck. Insert the ball of yarn for the head, and push it down as close as possible to the neck. Starting at the top of the bundle, using E that was knotted on, wrap the front and back of the head with E, then wrap yarn from the skein around creating a hat shape. Anchor and snip. Trim the hat with two French knots and a straight stitch embroidered in C.

Shoes: Wrap A ⅝in/1.5cm from the center out from each side of the shoe knot. Make the boot tops, after the legs have been wrapped with the pants color, by wrapping A over the pants, for 1in/2.5cm, building up layers at the top of the boot. Anchor and snip.

Pants: Use B to wrap the legs.

Arms: Wrap MC 30 times around a 7in/18cm board. Tie hands at each end; do not tie thumbs. Cover arms with wraps of F.

Jacket: Wrap F from the shoulder to the crotch, then around the opposite shoulder to the crotch in a V-shaped pattern five times on each side. Wrap yarn from the waist up to the underarm, then in a crisscross fashion around the waist and over each shoulder until the bodice is filled in completely. Wrap from the underarm to mid-thigh for the tunic. Anchor and snip. Bend the arms at the shoulders creating right angles so the arms hang as they do on a nutcracker. Wrap C around the neck and around the top of each sleeve, building up layers at top of each shoulder. Wrap two wraps at the bottom of each sleeve and one wrap ¼in/.6cm from the other wraps to create the cuff design. Anchor and snip. Thread a tapestry needle with one 24in/61cm piece of A. Embroider six French-knot buttons, connected by three straight stitches. Wrap A around the waist for the sash.

Hair: Wrap D 45 times around a 5in/12.5cm board. Knot into nine bunches of ten strands; secure the fringe down at the edge of the hat. Trim the hair.

Face: After stitching or knotting the features, anchor and snip all the loose ends of floss to secure and hide.

Thread a tapestry needle with four six-strand pieces of black embroidery floss; make a French knot eye. Rub on blush cheeks and gently draw Pigma-marker black eyebrows. Thread a tapestry needle with a doubled piece of body yarn. Anchor the yarn; make two stitches for the nose, then carry the yarn to the back of the head and anchor. Use one strand of yarn to sew two straight stitches for the mustache. Shape the mustache and anchor it with small stitches.

Sword: Wrap gray yarn four times around a 5in/12.5cm board. Tie bundle at one end with a 24in/61cm piece of gray yarn. Tie the other end with a 24in/61cm piece of C. Wrap the bottom (tip) of the sword with gray for 3in/7.5cm. Wrap the top of the sword with C creating a loop, then wrap down the top of the sword for ½in/1.25cm, creating a few layers. Tie a constrictor knot from a 12in/30.5cm piece of C at the top of the sword, and wrap one end of the yarn around one finger, creating a tab at the top of the sword. Use the remaining yarn to wrap around and cover this tab. Anchor and snip.

Sugar Plum Fairy

Adapted from The Nutcracker and the Mouse King by E. T. A. Hoffmann

FINISHED HEIGHT 12in/30.5cm

MATERIALS

Yarn

* Red Heart® Super Saver™ 7oz/198g, 364yds/333m (100% acrylic)—one skein each: #E300-313Aran (MC), #E300-373 Petal Pink (A), #E300-579 Pale Plum (B), and #E300-512 Turqua (C)

* Small amount of #E300-672 Spring Green (D)

* Red Heart® Boutique Sashay Sequins™ 3.5oz/100g, 20yds/18m (74% acrylic, 26% polyester)—one skein each: #7825-1989 Cotton Candy (E)

* Red Heart Soft® 5oz/141g, approx. 256yds/234m (100% acrylic)—one skein each: #E728-1882 Toast (F)

Other Tools

* Sharp scissors, a ruler, stiff cardboard, and a large, blunt-tipped tapestry needle

* Six-strand embroidery floss in black, white, dark aqua, and rose pink

* Powder blush or paint for cheeks

* Pigma #01 micron marker in brown

* Crochet hook (This will make it easier to form the knots for the hair.)

DOLL

Follow the basic directions for the Large Doll using MC. Do not wrap the legs with MC.

Shoes: Use A. Once the legs have been wrapped with B, fold an 18in/46cm piece of A in half and knot it to the back of the shoe at the halfway mark. Crisscross the ends of the yarn around the leg, and tie in the back to create a ballet slipper. Repeat for the other shoe.

Tights: Wrap the legs with B.

Bodice/Bloomers: Wrap with C.

Skirt: Cut one piece of E 3yds/2.75m long. Thread tapestry needle with an 18in/46cm piece of A and knot the end. Gather E yarn by running needle in and out of "ladder" at top edge of ruffle/tape yarn. Smooth gathers to make them even, then tie skirt around waist of doll. Anchor and snip.

Hair: The hair is rooted to the head with lark's head knots. Wrap F 140 times around a 12in/30.5cm board. Cut across the board evenly, creating 140 separate strands of yarn, each 24in/61cm long. There are 36 knots, each using three strands of yarn, forming a circle around the doll's head. Position the knots so they create the appearance of a natural hairline. Then make a row of five knots in front of the knots on the forehead to create bangs. Trim them to size. Gather the hair into a ponytail and, using an 18in/46cm piece of F, make a constrictor knot to hold the ponytail in place. Decorate the ponytail with a wrap of E. Anchor and snip. Trim the hair.

Face: Follow the basic directions for the Large Doll, using dark aqua floss to embroider the colored part of the eye.

Adapted from The Nutcracker and the Mouse King by E. T. A. Hoffmann

FINISHED HEIGHT 12in/30.5cm

MATERIALS

Yarn

* Premier® Yarns Deborah Norville Collection™ Everyday® Soft Worsted 4oz/113g, 203yds/186m (100% anti-pilling acrylic)—one skein each: #ED100-02 Cream (MC), #102 Black (A), #1009 Royal Blue (B), #1007 Really Red (C), #1028 Mustard (D)

* Premier® Yarns Deborah Norville Collection™ Serenity® Sock Solids 1.76oz/50g, 230yds/210m (50% wool, 25% nylon, 25% rayon)—one skein each: # 5012 Black (E)

Other Tools

* Sharp scissors, a ruler, stiff cardboard, and a large, blunt-tipped tapestry needle

* Six-strand embroidery floss in black, white, green, and rose pink

* Powder blush or paint for cheeks

* Pigma #01 micron marker in black

* Crochet hook (This will make it easier to form the knots for the hair.)

DOLL

Follow the basic directions for the Large Doll using MC. Do not wrap the legs with MC.

Shoes: Use A; make the shoes following the basic directions. Make the boot tops, after the legs have been wrapped with the pants color, by wrapping A over the pants for 2in/5cm, building up layers at the top of the boot. Repeat for the other leg. Anchor and snip.

Pants: Use B to wrap the legs and to form the hips.

Jacket: Using C, wrap the yarn from the shoulder to the crotch, then around opposite the shoulder to the crotch in a V-shaped pattern eight times on each side. Wrap the yarn from the waist up to the underarm, then in a crisscross pattern around the waist and over each shoulder until the bodice is filled in completely. Wrap from the underarm to mid-thigh for the tunic. Wrap each arm with ¼in/.6cm of A at the wrists, then wrap from the wrist to the shoulder with C. Wrap D a few times around the neck and around the top of each sleeve, building up layers at the top of each shoulder. Anchor and snip. Thread a tapestry needle with one 24in/61cm piece of A. Embroider six French-knot buttons, connected by three straight stitches. Wrap A around the waist for the sash.

Hair: (The Prince's hair is made in two parts.)
The hair is rooted to the head at the hairline with lark's head knots; a fringe is sewn to the crown of the head for additional coverage. Note that sock weight yarn requires the use of more knots for coverage. Wrap E 180 times around a 5in/12.5cm board. Cut across the board evenly, creating 180 strands of yarn 10in/25cm long. There are 60 knots, each using three strands of yarn, forming a circle around the doll's head. Position the knots so they create the appearance of a natural hairline. The Prince has 40 knots around his head, and a double row of knots along the front. Then, following the basic directions, make a fringe by wrapping E 120 times around a 5in/12.5cm board. Knot across the fringe, making ten bunches of 12 strands. Cut the fringe open and fold in half. Sew the center part, and stitch it down to the crown of the head. Trim all hair.

Face: Follow the basic directions for the Large Doll, using green floss to embroider the colored part of the eye.

Hansel

From the German fairy tale "Hansel and Gretel"

FINISHED HEIGHT 11in/28cm

MATERIALS

Yarn

* Rowan Pure Wool Superwash Worsted 3.53oz/100g, approx. 219yd/200m (100% superwash wool)—one skein each: #102 Soft Cream (MC), #110 Umber (A), #152 Oats (B), #144 Mallard (C), #153 Light Navy (D), #132 Buttercup (E)

Other Tools

* Sharp scissors, a ruler, stiff cardboard, and a large, blunt-tipped tapestry needle

* Six-strand embroidery floss in black, white, blue, and rose pink

* Powder blush or paint for cheeks

* Pigma #01 micron marker in brown

* Crochet hook (This will make it easier to form the knots for the hair.)

DOLL

Follow the basic directions for the Large Doll using MC.

Shoes: Use A.

Legs: Wrap legs with MC. Make socks by covering 1in/2.5cm at the bottom of the legs with wraps of D.

Shirt: Using B, wrap yarn around the upper arm 20 times, then wrap the yarn evenly covering the arm to the wrist and then back up to the shoulder, continuing to wrap until the arm and shoulder are smooth. Anchor and snip; repeat for the other arm. Thread a tapestry needle with a 24in/61cm piece of A, and embroider two French-knot buttons.

Lederhosen: Wrap the top of the leg for 1¾in/4.5cm with three layers of C. Repeat for the other leg. Wrap yarn around the waist a number of times, then wrap around the thighs in a figure-8 fashion until the backside is covered. Wrap yarn around the waist to mask the previous wraps, then wrap the yarn down the legs until the shorts are smooth. Anchor and snip. Cut three 24in/61cm pieces of D and braid them together. Fold the braid in half, and secure the fold to the center back of the doll at the waistband. Bring the ends of the braid over the shoulders and tuck them into the waistband, trimming to fit, to make the suspenders. Wrap one piece of D around the suspenders in the front; anchor and snip.

Hair: (Hansel's hair is made in 2 parts.) The hair is rooted to the head at the hairline with lark's head knots; a fringe is sewn to the crown of the head for additional coverage. Wrap E 80 times around a 5in/12.5cm board. Cut across the board evenly, creating 80 strands of yarn, 10in/25cm long. There are 40 knots, each using two strands of yarn, forming a circle around the doll's head. Position the knots so they create the appearance of a natural hairline. Hansel has 30 knots around his head, and a double row of knots along the front. Then, make a fringe, following the basic directions for the hair, by wrapping E 50 times around a 5in/12.5cm board. Knot across the fringe, making ten bunches of ten strands. Cut the fringe open and fold in half. Sew the center part, and stitch it down to the crown of the head. Trim all hair. Separate some of the front strands by teasing with a tapestry needle.

Face: Follow the basic directions for the Large Doll, using blue floss to embroider the colored part of the eye.

Gretel

From the German fairy tale "Hansel and Gretel"

FINISHED HEIGHT 11in/28cm

MATERIALS

Yarn

* Rowan Pure Wool Superwash Worsted, 3.53oz/100g, approx. 219yd/200m (100% superwash wool)—one skein each: #102 Soft Cream (MC), #107 Chestnut (A), #152 Oats (B), #101 Ivory (C), #129 Apple (D), #117 Raspberry (E), and #132 Buttercup (F)

Other Tools

* Sharp scissors, a ruler, stiff cardboard, and a large, blunt-tipped tapestry needle

* Six-strand embroidery floss in black, white, blue, and rose pink

* Powder blush or paint for cheeks

* Pigma #01 micron marker in brown

DOLL

Follow the basic directions for the Large Doll.

Shoes: Use A.

Legs/Tights: Using B, wrap 4½in/11.5cm from the ankle to the crotch.

Blouse/Upper Body: Use C. Follow the basic directions, then attach the yarn to the top of the right arm, and wrap six times at the top to build the shoulder. Wrap the yarn evenly 1in/2.5cm from the shoulder to create a short sleeve. Wrap from the bottom of the sleeve to the shoulder with four more layers of yarn. Anchor and snip. Repeat for the left arm. Cut two 12in/30.5cm pieces of E, and anchor at the right front hip; bring the yarn around the back of the neck and anchor and snip at the left front hip to make straps. Wrap a thick sash using A.

Bloomers: Use D.

Skirt: Cut 48 pieces of D and 12 pieces of E, 9in/23cm long. Cut a 40in/102cm piece of D and fold it in half. Anchor it to a board and use it as a foundation for a lark's head knot fringe. Each knot is made up of three pieces of yarn. Make the fringe in this sequence: eight knots of D, four knots of E, eight knots of D. Trim the skirt evenly to 3½in/9cm or to desired length. Tie the skirt around the waist.

Hair: Follow the basic directions for the hair; use F wrapped 120 times around a 9in/23cm board. Sew hair to the head and trim evenly. Braid the front pieces of hair using six pieces of yarn. Repeat for other side. Tie the two braids behind the head in a low ponytail. Create a headband by making a braid from 12 pieces of F, each 24in/61cm long. Wrap the band around the hair, and tie at the back of the head under the hair. Trim the ends. Cut one piece of D and tie a bow around the braid. Trim ends.

Face: Follow the basic directions for the Large Doll, using blue floss to embroider the colored part of the eye.

Cinderella—Tatters

From the fairy tale "Cinderella"

FINISHED HEIGHT 12in/30.5cm

MATERIALS

Yarn

* Lion Brand® Yarns Pound of Love 16oz/454g, 1050yds/932m (100% premium acrylic)—one skein each: #550-099 Soft Cream (MC)

* Lion Brand® Yarns Vanna's Choice® 3.5oz/100g, 170yds/156m (100% acrylic)—one skein each: #860-124 Toffee (A), #860-126 Chocolate (B)

* Lion Brand® Yarns Vanna's Choice® 3oz/85g, 145yds/133m (92% acrylic, 8% rayon)—one skein each: #401 Grey Marble (C)

* Lion Brand® Yarns Vanna's Choice® 3oz/85g skein, 145yds/133m (100% acrylic)—one skein each: #860-306 Tangerine Mist (D)

* Lion Brand® Yarns Babysoft®, 5oz/140g, 459yds/420m (60% acrylic, 40% nylon)—one skein each: #920-160 Lemonade (E), #920-157 Pastel Yellow (F)

* Small amounts of green and brown yarn for hair band

* Scraps of dark brown, beige, and gold yarn for broom

Other Tools

* Sharp scissors, a ruler, stiff cardboard, and a large, blunt-tipped tapestry needle

* Six-strand embroidery floss in black, white, and rose pink

* Powder blush or paint for cheeks

* Pigma #01 micron marker in brown

DOLL

Follow the basic directions for the Large Doll using MC.

Shoes: Use A.

Tights and Bloomers: Wrap the legs with C. Wrap the hips using D, then wrap snugly around the waist two or three times; anchor and snip.

Blouse/Upper Body Color/Apron Top: Wrap the arms and body with C, anchor and snip. Wrap B in a crisscross fashion four times over each shoulder, and then firmly wrap around the waist ten times. Anchor and snip.

Skirt: Cut 40 pieces of D and 6 pieces of B, 12in/30.5cm long. Cut a 24in/61cm piece of D and fold it in half. Anchor it to a board and use it as a foundation for a lark's head knot fringe. Using two 12in/30.5cm pieces at a time, work ten lark's head knots of D, then three knots of B, then ten knots of D. Tie fringe securely around the waist. Trim.

Face: Follow the basic directions for the Large Doll, using black floss to embroider the colored part of the eye.

Hair: Wrap one strand each of E and F held together 90 times around a 9in/23cm board. Following the basic hair directions, knot into ten bunches of 18 strands each. Trim some front strands for bangs. Wrap green yarn around hair five or six times for the hair band. Cut four 5in/12.5cm pieces of brown yarn; knot around the hair band and trim.

BROOM

Wrap beige yarn 24 times around a 3in/7.5cm board. Tie at top to make a bundle. Cut 12 pieces of dark brown yarn 9in/23cm. Pull the pieces through the top of the bundle and fold them in half. Using dark brown yarn, secure the end and wrap the handle of the broom firmly. Anchor and snip. Tie on one piece of gold yarn, and wrap it around the top of the broom several times. Tie the ends together, anchor and snip. Cut bottom of the broom bundle; trim.

Cinderella—Gown

From the fairy tale "Cinderella"

FINISHED HEIGHT 11in/28cm

MATERIALS

Yarn

* Deborah Norville Collection™ Everyday® Soft Worsted 4oz/113g, 203yds/186m (100% anti-pilling acrylic)—one skein each: #ED100-02 Cream (MC), #ED100-05 Baby Blue (A)

* Premier® Yarns Spangle™ 1.76oz/50g, 164 yds/150m (75% nylon, 25% metallic)—one ball each: #11-208 Sparkling Water (B)

* Premier® Yarns Moonstone 1.75oz/50g, 93yds/85m (75% polyamide, 25% polyester)—one ball each: #96-09 Bacchus (C)

* Premier® Yarns EverSoft® 3oz/85g, approx. 158yds/144.5m (100% acrylic)—one skein each: #0001 Daisy (D), #0002 Sunflower (E)

Other Tools

* Sharp scissors, a ruler, stiff cardboard, and a large, blunt-tipped tapestry needle

* Six-strand embroidery floss in black, white, blue, and rose pink

* Powder blush or paint for cheeks

* Pigma #01 micron marker in brown

DOLL

Follow the basic directions for the Large Doll.

Shoes: Use B.

Blouse/Bloomers: Use A. Wrap five times around each upper arm for sleeves.

Skirt: Using one strand each of A and C held together, make 60 wraps around a 9in/23cm board. Cut across the wraps to make 120 strands for fringe. Cut a 24in/61cm piece of A and fold it in half. Anchor it to a board and use it as a foundation for a lark's head knot fringe of ten bunches of 12 strands each. Tie the skirt around the waist, and secure it to the doll with a few stitches or knots if necessary. Trim the fringe.

Hair: Follow the basic directions for the hair, using one strand each of D and E held together and wrapped 60 times. Make a tiara/headband by twisting together two 60in/152cm strands of B and one 60in/152cm strand of C. Attach the strands to a table or doorknob and twist them firmly until they double back on themselves. Fold the length in half and let it coil into a rope. Tie the headband on behind the hair.

Face: Follow the basic directions for the Large Doll, using blue floss to embroider the colored part of the eye.

Prince Charming

From the fairy tale "Cinderella"

FINISHED HEIGHT 12in/30.5cm

MATERIALS

Yarn

* Lion Brand® Vanna's Choice® 3.5oz/100g, 170yds/156m (100% acrylic)—one skein each: #098 Fisherman (MC), #153 Black (A), #108 Bluebell (B), #100 White (C), #126 Chocolate (D), #125 Taupe (E)

* Lion Brand® Glitterspun® approx. 16ft/5m (80% polyester, 20% nylon)—one card each: #605-170 Gold (F)

* Small amount of red yarn (G) for sash

Other Materials

* Sharp scissors, a ruler, stiff cardboard, and a large, blunt-tipped tapestry needle

* Six-strand embroidery floss in black, white, and rose pink

* Powder blush or paint for cheeks

* Pigma #01 micron marker in brown

* Crochet hook (This will make it easier to form the knots for the hair.)

DOLL

Follow the basic directions for the Large Doll.

Shoes: Use A; make the shoes following the basic directions. Make boot tops, after the legs have been wrapped with the pants color, by wrapping A over the pants for 2in/5cm, building up layers at the top of the boot. Repeat for the other leg. Anchor and snip.

Pants: Use B.

Shirt: Follow the basic directions using C. Make sleeves by wrapping B yarn around the wrist for ½in/1.25cm to create a cuff, then wrap the arms from cuff to shoulder using C. Layer the wraps of yarn to create the shoulder. Repeat for the other arm. Wrap C around hips until tunic is desired length. Thread a tapestry needle with F and make two rows of four French knots for buttons. Wrap F around neck for the collar, and then wrap around hips for the belt. Wrap G around from left shoulder to right hip eight times to make the sash. Switch to F and wrap two wraps on each side of the sash to create a border. Anchor and snip.

Hair: (made in two parts.) The hair is rooted to the head at the hairline with lark's head knots; a fringe is sewn to the crown of the head for additional coverage. Wrap one strand each of D and E held together, 40 times around a 5in/12.5cm board. Cut across the board evenly, creating 80 strands of yarn 10in/25cm long. There are 40 knots, each using two strands of yarn (one of each color), forming a circle around the doll's head. Position the knots so they create the appearance of a natural hairline. The Prince has 30 knots around his head, and a double row of knots along the front. Then, make a fringe following the basic directions for the hair by wrapping one strand each of D and E held together 50 times around a 5in/12.5cm board. Knot across the fringe, making ten bunches of ten strands each. Cut the fringe open and fold it in half. Sew the center part, and stitch it down to the crown of the head. Trim all hair.

Phinye

From a West African folktale

FINISHED HEIGHT 11in/28cm

MATERIALS

Yarn

* Red Heart® Super Saver™ 7 oz/198g, approx. 364 yds/333m (100% acrylic)—one skein each: #E300-360 Café Latte (MC), #E300-0256 Carrot (A), #E300-235 Lemon (B)

* Red Heart® Boutique Sashay Boho™ 3.5oz/100g, approx. 23yds/21m (69% acrylic, 31% polyester)—one skein each: #E782B-1987 Saucy (C)

* Red Heart® Heart & Sole™ 1.76oz/50g, approx. 187yds/171m (73% wool, 27% nylon)—one skein each: #E840-3112 Black (D)

OTHER MATERIALS

* Sharp scissors, a ruler, stiff cardboard, and a large, blunt-tipped tapestry needle

* Six-strand embroidery floss in black, white, brown, and rose pink

* Powder blush or paint for cheeks

* Pigma #01 micron marker in black

DOLL

Follow the basic directions for the Large Doll using MC.

Shoes: Use A.

Upper Body/Bloomers: Use B.

Skirt: Wrap C around bodice down to hips until covered. Wrap one time over right shoulder; anchor and snip.

Hair: Use D wrapped 150 times over a 9in/23cm board. Make ten bunches of 15 strands each. Cut a 36in/91cm piece of C and wrap it a few times around the head to create the head wrap.

Face: Follow the basic directions for the Large Doll, using brown floss to embroider the colored part of the eye.

Princess Kaguya

From "The Tale of the Bamboo Cutter," a tenth-century Japanese folktale

FINISHED HEIGHT 12in/30.5cm

MATERIALS

Yarn

* Cascade Yarns® Elysian 3.5oz/100g, approx. 219yds/200m (60% superwash merino wool, 40% acrylic)—one skein each: #18 White Swan (MC), #03 Pirate Black (A)

* Cascade Yarns® Venezia Sport 3.5oz/100g, approx. 307.5 yds/281m (70% merino wool, 30% silk)—one skein each: #197 Spring Green (B), #177 Orchid Haze (C)

Other Tools

* Sharp scissors, a ruler, stiff cardboard, and a large, blunt-tipped tapestry needle

* Six-strand embroidery floss in black, white, brown, magenta, and rose pink

* Powder blush or paint for cheeks

* Pigma #01 micron marker in brown

DOLL

Follow the basic directions for the Large Doll using MC.

Shoes: Use A.

Kimono Top: Wrap bodice with B, but do not anchor and snip. Attach C to right hip and wrap eight times from the right hip over the left shoulder, then bring yarn behind neck and wrap eight times from right shoulder to left hip. Anchor and snip. Wrap eight times with B below the eight wraps just made with C (from right shoulder to left hip). Wrap two layers of B for sleeves, starting ¼ in/.6cm above hands and making extra wraps to build up shoulders and cuffs. Anchor and snip all yarn.

Bloomers/Tights: Wrap legs and arms with MC. To make the tights, wrap over the legs with two layers of B, wrapping from ¼in/.6cm above the shoe up to the hips, and then wrap bloomers with B.

Kimono Skirt: Cut 44 pieces of B and 4 pieces of C, each 12in/30.5cm long. Cut 24in/61cm piece of B and fold it in half. Anchor it to a board and use it as a foundation for a lark's head knot fringe. Make fringe of 24 knots with two strands of yarn. Fringe sequence is seven knots of B, two knots of C, fifteen knots of B. Trim fringe to 4½in/11.5cm. Tie skirt around waist, lining up the stripe of C with the left hip and the color C wraps from the bodice.

Obi Sash: Wrap a sash 1in/2.5cm high around the waist using C. Cut a 48in/122cm piece of magenta six-strand embroidery floss. Attach it to a table and twist it until it doubles back on itself to form a rope. Knot both ends, and wrap in a crisscross fashion around the sash. Knot to secure, then trim the ends.

Hair: Use A, wrapped 140 times around a 9in/23cm board. Attach to head following basic directions for hair, and then pull some pieces of hair forward and trim for bangs. Gather first ten pieces of hair on each side and, using a piece of A, tie the pieces together in a low ponytail, under the rest of the hair. Secure at the back of head. Arrange the rest of the hair. Cut a 30in/76cm piece of magenta six-strand embroidery floss. Pinch a clump of 18 pieces of hair from the top right side of the head. Use the floss to wrap a 1in/2.5cm section of hair starting 2½in/6cm from the bottom. Anchor and snip. Repeat for left side. Knot the two wrapped sections in a simple overhand knot at the top of the head.

Face: Follow the basic directions for the Large Doll, using brown floss to embroider the colored part of the eye.

The Lamb

From "The Little Lamb," a Sicilian folktale

FINISHED HEIGHT 11in/28cm (head to toe, stretched)

MATERIALS

Yarn

* Lion Brand® Vanna's Choice® 3.5oz/100g, (170yds/156m (100% acrylic)—one skein each: #860-100 White (MC), #860-153 Black (A)

* Lion Brand® Homespun® 6oz/170g, approx. 185 yds/169m (98% acrylic, 2% polyester)—one skein each: #790-300 Hepplewhite (B)

* Scraps of pink and gray yarn

Other Tools

* Sharp scissors, a ruler, stiff cardboard, and a large, blunt-tipped tapestry needle

* Six-strand embroidery floss in black, white, and rose pink

* Powder blush or paint for cheeks

DOLL

The lamb is made following the basic directions, and in the same sequence, as for the Large Doll, but hooves are made instead of shoes and hands. The foreleg piece is made instead of the arm bundle.

Head/Body/Leg Bundles: (**Make 2**) Follow the basic directions using 65 strands of MC. The legs will form the hind legs of the lamb. Make a ball 7in/18cm in circumference; fill the head with the ball, leaving room to insert the ears.

Earpiece: (Make 1) Wrap B 20 times around a 7in/18cm board. Tie with a constrictor knot at each end, using a 36in/91cm piece of B. Wrap yarn around the bundle for 3in/7.5cm at each end, as if to wrap for shoes. Fold each ear in half at the center point and, working with the yarn from the skein, secure each end and wrap around the rest of

the bundle. Anchor and snip. Insert the piece into the head, over the ball of yarn, and as close to the constrictor knot as possible.

Hind Legs/Hooves: Make the hooves following the basic directions for the shoes using A. Wrap the legs using MC, building up the layers at the upper thigh.

Forelegs Piece/Hooves: (Make 1) Wrap A 65 times around a 9in/23cm board. Tie at each end with a constrictor knot, and wrap following the basic directions for the shoes. Switch to MC and wrap the bundle until it is firm and fully covered. Insert it into the body and tie a piece of yarn around body to secure.

Upper Body and Lower Body: Before wrapping the body, make a ball with a 5in/12.5cm circumference from MC and insert it into the belly of the lamb. Using MC from the skein, wrap the body following the basic directions, building up the wraps until the body is firm. Switch to B. The finished circumference around each thigh will be 6in/15cm, around the hips 10in/25cm, and around the belly 9½in/24cm.

Top Tuft of Hair: Wrap B six times around a 3in/7.5cm board. Remove the loops carefully and tie in the middle to secure, making a "butterfly" shape. Slide this piece under the constrictor knot at the top of the head. Fan out the loops.

Tail: Cut two 4in/10cm pieces of B. Tie them in a knot on the backside of lamb. Trim to size.

Face: Follow the basic directions for the face, but do not embroider a colored part of the eye. The nose is three straight stitches of pink wool.

Scarf: Cut six 24in/61cm pieces of gray yarn. Make a braid using two pieces of yarn for each section. Knot 1½in/4cm from each end. Trim ends for fringe and tie around the lamb's neck in a bow.

Princess in Gold

From "The Little Lamb," a Sicilian folktale

FINISHED HEIGHT 11in/28cm

MATERIALS

Yarn

* Lion Brand® Vanna's Choice® 3.5oz/100g, approx. 170yds/156m (100% acrylic)—one skein each: #860-098 Fisherman (MC), #860-153 Black (A), #860-158 Mustard (B), #860-126 Chocolate (C), #860-127 Espresso (D)

* Lion Brand® Vanna's Glamour® 1.75oz/50g, 170yds/156m (96% acrylic, 4% other fiber)—one skein each: #861-171 Gold (E)

* Lion Brand® Glitterspun® approx. 16ft/5m (80% polyester, 20% nylon)—one card each: #605-170 Gold (F)

Other Tools

* Sharp scissors, a ruler, stiff cardboard, and a large, blunt-tipped tapestry needle

* Six-strand embroidery floss in black, white, brown, and rose pink

* Powder blush or paint for cheeks

* Pigma #01 micron marker in brown

DOLL

Follow the basic directions for the Large Doll using MC.

Shoes: Use A.

Bloomers: Use B.

Bodice: Use E. Make the sleeves by wrapping the yarn around the upper arms for 1in/2.5cm.

Skirt: Cut 52 pieces of B and E, 14in/35.5cm long. Cut a 24in/61cm piece of B and fold it in half. Anchor it to a board and use it as a foundation for a lark's head knot fringe of 26 knots, using one piece of B and one piece of E. Trim the ends to 5in/12.5cm. Tie the skirt around the waist. Make a sash by wrapping B around the waist for 1in/2.5cm.

Hair: Follow the basic directions using one strand each of C and D held together; wrap 60 times.

Tiara: Cut three 36in/92cm pieces of F. Holding the three pieces of yarn together as one, either crochet a 3½in/9cm chain, or create a finger chain by making a loose slip knot loop around two fingers and pulling one loop after another through the loop just made. Leave a tail at the end and tie onto the hair. Alternatively, the tiara could be braided.

Face: Follow the basic directions for the Large Doll, using brown floss to embroider the colored part of the eye.

Gingerbread Boy

From the 1875 story "The Gingerbread Boy"

FINISHED HEIGHT 7in/18cm

MATERIALS

Yarn

* Premier® Yarns Parfait™ 3.5oz/100g, approx. 192yds/172m (100% polyester)— one skein each: #3002 Toffee (MC)

* Small amounts of toffee, white, black, and red yarn

Other Tools

* Sharp scissors, a ruler, stiff cardboard, and a large, blunt-tipped tapestry needle

DOLL

Follow the basic directions for the Large Doll. Wrap two head/body/leg bundles, 70 times each around a 7in/18cm board. Fill the head with a toffee-colored yarn ball that is 6in/15cm in circumference.

Shoes/Legs: Make the feet using MC, following basic directions for shoes. Wrap the legs with MC. Decorate the ankles with wraps of white yarn.

Arms: Make the arm bundle by wrapping MC 20 times around a 6in/15cm board. Tie at each end with a constrictor knot for the hands, but do not make thumbs. Wrap the arms with MC. Decorate the arms with wraps of white yarn at the wrists.

Body: Wrap the body, hip, and torso with MC, building up the wraps until the shape is pleasing. Wrap yarn around the lower body so that only 1in/2.5cm of the legs above the ankles shows. Decorate the body with three French knots made from white yarn.

Face: Embroider two large French-knot eyes using black yarn.

Scarf: Make a 12in/30.5cm braid using three pieces of red yarn. Knot at each end to secure, and tie around the neck in a bow.

The Italian version of "Rapunzel"

FINISHED HEIGHT 11in/28cm

MATERIALS

Yarn

* Lion Brand® Vanna's Choice® 3.5oz/100g skein, 170yds/156m, (100% acrylic)—one skein each: #860-098 Fisherman (MC), #860-151 Charcoal Grey (A), #860-101 Light Pink (B), #860-149 Silver Grey (C), #860-171 Fern (D)

* Lion Brand® Babysoft® 5oz/141g, approx. 459yds/420m (60% acrylic, 40% polyamid)— one skein each: #920-157 Pastel Yellow (E), #920-160 Lemonade (F)

Other Tools

* Sharp scissors, a ruler, stiff cardboard, and a large, blunt-tipped tapestry needle

* Six-strand embroidery floss in black, white, brown, and rose pink

* Powder blush or paint for cheeks

* Pigma #01 micron marker in brown

DOLL

Follow the basic directions for the Large Doll, using MC. Do not wrap the arms or legs with MC.

Shoes: Use A.

Tights/Bloomers: Use C.

Bodice: Use B. Make sleeves by wrapping the arms from the wrist to the shoulder.

Skirt: Cut 50 pieces of C, 18in/46cm long. Cut a 24in/61cm piece of C and fold it in half. Anchor it to a board and use it as a foundation for a lark's head knot fringe of 25 knots, each made with two pieces of cut yarn. Tie the skirt around the waist. Make a sash by wrapping A around the waist for ½in/1.25cm.

Hair: Make the hair as for the Large Doll, wrapping one strand each of E and F held together 100 times around a 16in/41cm board. Attach to the head and braid one front section.

Flower Vine: Cut a 160in/406cm piece of D. Fold it in half and attach it to a table or doorknob. Twist the yarn until it doubles back upon itself. Cut the yarn from the anchored end, and knot it to make a rope.

Flowers: (Make 3) Wrap B around two fingers four times and use a 12in/30.5cm piece of D to knot in the center and secure. Remove the flower carefully from the fingers and arrange the loops so they are spread out and similar in size. Tie the flowers onto the vine with the ends from the center knot. Trim ends. Attach the rope, with the double end on top, to the hair at the top of the braid. Wrap around the doll's hair.

Face: Follow the basic directions for the Large Doll, using brown floss to embroider the colored part of the eye.

From "Thumbelina" by Hans Christian Andersen

FINISHED HEIGHT 7½in/19cm

MATERIALS

Yarn

* Cascade Yarns® 220 Superwash® 3.5oz/100g, approx. 220yds/200m (100% superwash wool)—one skein each: #817 Aran (MC)

* Cascade Yarns® 220 Superwash® Sport 1.75oz/50g, approx. 136.5yds/125m (100% superwash merino wool)—)one hank each: #897 Baby Denim (A), #820 Lemon (B), #877 Golden (C)

* Cascade Yarns® 220 Superwash® Sport Multis 1.75oz/50gr, approx.. 136.5yds/125m (100% superwash merino wool)—one hank each: #103 Baby (D)

Other Tools

* Sharp scissors, a ruler, stiff cardboard, and a large, blunt-tipped tapestry needle

* Six-strand embroidery floss in black, white, blue, and rose pink

* Powder blush or paint for cheeks

* Pigma #01 micron marker in brown

* Crochet hook (This will make it easier to form the knots for the hair.)

DOLL

Using MC, make two head/body/leg bundles, following the basic directions for the Large Doll and wrapping the yarn 50 times around a 9in/23cm board. Fill the head with a 6½in/16.5cm circumference ball of scrap yarn.

Shoes: Using A, wrap ¾in/2cm on either side of the center knot following the basic directions for the Large Doll.

Arms: Wrap MC 35 times around a 6in/15cm board. Make the arms following the basic directions for the Large Doll. Use five strands for the thumbs.

Shirt/Bloomers: Use B.

Skirt: Cut 60 pieces of D, 6in/15cm long. Cut a 24in/61cm piece of C and fold it in half. Anchor it to a board and use it as a foundation for a lark's head knot fringe of 20 knots, each made of three pieces of cut yarn. The belt is made by making two decorative rows of lark's head knots across the top of the fringe using A. The rows of knots are made in the same manner as the rows of knots used to make the hair (see the basic instructions for the Large Doll). Trim the fringe evenly and tie the skirt around the waist.

Hair: Cut 105 pieces of C, 18in/46cm long, and make 35 lark's head knots around the entire hairline, using three pieces of yarn for each knot. Position the knots so that they create the appearance of a natural hairline. Cut 12 pieces of C, 3in/7.5cm long and make bangs by making three lark's head knots of two pieces of yarn each, on the center forehead of the doll. Pull the hair into a ponytail and secure it with a 12in/30.5cm piece of C, tied into a constrictor knot. Cut a 12in/30.5cm piece of A and tie it into a bow around the base of the ponytail.

Face: Follow the basic directions for the Large Doll, using blue floss to embroider the colored part of the eye.

Flower Prince

From "Thumbelina" by Hans Christian Andersen

FINISHED HEIGHT 7½in/19cm

MATERIALS

Yarn

* Cascade Yarns® 220 Superwash® 3.5oz/100g, approx. 220yds/200m (100% superwash wool)—one skein each: #817 Aran (MC)

* Cascade Yarns® 220 Superwash® Sport 1.75 oz/50g, approx. 136.5yds/125m (100% superwash merino wool)—one hank each: #223 Juniper (A), #841 Moss (B), #224 Methyl Blue (C), #181 Mocha (D)

* Small amounts of red yarn for flower

Other Tools

* Sharp scissors, a ruler, stiff cardboard, and a large, blunt-tipped tapestry needle

* Six-strand embroidery floss in black, white, green, and rose pink

* Powder blush or paint for cheeks

* Pigma #01 micron marker in brown

* Crochet hook (This will make it easier to form the knots for the hair.)

DOLL

Using MC, make two head/body/leg bundles, following the basic directions for the Large Doll and wrapping the yarn 50 times around a 9in/23cm board. Fill the head with a 6½in/16.5cm circumference ball of scrap yarn. Do not wrap the arms or legs with MC.

Shoes: Using A, wrap ¾in/2cm on either side of the center knot, following the basic directions for the Large Doll.

Arms: Wrap MC 35 times around a 6in/15cm board. Make the arms following the basic directions for the Large Doll. Use five strands for each thumb. Do not wrap the arms with MC.

Tunic: Use C. Wrap the body as directed in the basic directions, and then wrap from the wrist to the shoulder, building up layers at the shoulder. Repeat for the other arm. Wrap from the waist to the hips to make the tunic. Switch to B and wrap the yarn in a crisscross fashion 12 times on each side from the shoulder to the waist to create the sash. Wrap red yarn around two fingers, and tie a knot in the center to make a flower. Cut the wrapped yarn on each end to create a pompom. Tease the yarn strands with the tip of a needle to separate. Wrap B around the waist two times for a belt. Use a piece of B to tie the flower to the belt. Clip the ends of the yarn to 1in/2.5cm and tease with the tip of a needle to gently separate plies and to create leaves.

Hair: (The Prince's hair is made in two parts.) The hair is rooted to the head at the hairline with lark's head knots. Note that sport weight yarn requires the use of more knots for coverage. Wrap D 200 times around a 3in/7.5cm board. Cut across the board evenly, creating 200 strands of yarn 6in/15cm long. There are 35 knots, each using two strands of yarn, forming a circle around the doll's head. Position the knots so they create the appearance of a natural hairline. The Prince has 35 knots around his head, and a double row of knots along the front. Fill in the rest of the scalp with knots, adding more yarn if necessary. Trim all hair.

Face: Follow the basic directions for the Large Doll, using green floss to embroider the colored part of the eye.

Wings: Use B. Cut a 60in/152cm piece of yarn. Fold it in half once, then in half again, creating a 15in/38cm piece of four strands of yarn. Anchor one end of this piece to a table or board using a bulldog clip or tape. Using yarn from the skein, cover the entire piece of yarn with half hitch knots, pushing them together so that the cord created is strong. Fold the cord into a figure-8 shape, placing the cut ends in the center where the two loops meet. Wrap the center section to secure and hide any loose ends. Secure to the doll with a few knots or stitches.

Robin Hood

From English folklore

FINISHED HEIGHT 11½in/29cm

MATERIALS

YARN

* Lion Brand® Vanna's Choice® 3.5oz/100g, approx. 170yds/156m (100% acrylic)—one skein each: #860-098 Fisherman (MC), #860-127 Espresso (A), #860-172 Kelly Green (B), #860-171 Fern (C), #860-124 Toffee (D), #860-126 Chocolate (E), #860-125 Taupe (F)

* Lion Brand® Amazing® Yarn 1.75oz/50g, 147yds/135m (53% wool, 47% acrylic)—one skein each: #825-202 Rainforest (G)

* Small amounts of gold yarn

OTHER TOOLS

* Sharp scissors, a ruler, stiff cardboard, and a large, blunt-tipped tapestry needle

* Six-strand embroidery floss in black, white, medium blue, and rose pink

* Powder blush or paint for cheeks

* Pigma #01 micron marker in brown

* Crochet hook (This will make it easier to form the knots for the hair.)

DOLL

Follow the basic directions for the Large Doll. Use MC for the head/body/leg bundle. Use F to make the arm bundle. Do not wrap the arms or legs with MC.

Shoes: Use A.

Legs: Use B.

Arms/Gauntlets: Wrap arms with C. Make the gauntlets by wrapping with F for 1in/2.5cm starting at the wrist. Build up layers of yarn to form the cuff.

Tunic/Bloomers: Use G.

Fringe: Cut 56 pieces of G, 6in/15cm long. Cut a 24in/61cm piece of G and fold it in half. Anchor it to a board and use it as a foundation for a lark's head

knot fringe of 28 knots, each using two strands of yarn. Trim the fringe and tie it around the waist.

Sash and belt: Wrap gold yarn a number of times around the waist to form the belt, then wrap from the waist over the shoulder to form the sash. Anchor and snip.

Hair: (Robin Hood's hair is made in two parts.) The hair is rooted to the head at the hairline with lark's head knots; a fringe is sewn to the crown of the head for additional coverage. Wrap one strand each of D and E held together, 40 times around a 5in/12.5cm board. Cut across the board evenly, creating 80 strands of yarn, 10in/25cm long. There are 40 knots, each using two strands of yarn (one of each color), forming a circle around the doll's head. Position the knots so they create the appearance of a natural hairline. Robin Hood has 30 knots around his head, and a double row of knots along the front. Then, make a fringe, following the basic directions, by wrapping one strand each of D and E held together 50 times around a 5in/12.5cm board. Knot across the fringe, making ten bunches of ten strands each. Cut the fringe open and fold in half. Sew the center part, and stitch it down to the crown of the head. Trim all hair.

Face: Follow the basic directions for the Large Doll, using medium blue floss to embroider the colored part of the eye.

Maid Marian

From English folklore

FINISHED HEIGHT 11in/28cm

MATERIALS

YARN

* Rowan Pure Wool Superwash Worsted 3.53oz/100g, approx. 219yd/200m (100% superwash wool)—one skein each: #102 Soft Cream (MC), #109 Black (A), #121 Morello (B), #151 Rose Pink (C), #107 Chestnut (D)

* Small amounts of gold yarn

OTHER MATERIALS

* Sharp scissors, a ruler, stiff cardboard, and a large, blunt-tipped tapestry needle

* Six-strand embroidery floss in black, white, green, and rose pink

* Metallic gold embroidery floss and braid

* Powder blush or paint for cheeks

* Pigma #01 micron marker in brown

DOLL

Follow the basic instructions for the Large Doll, using MC. Do not wrap the arms or legs with MC.

Shoes: Use A.

Tights/Bloomers: Use B.

Blouse: Use B. Wrap the arms with B, then switch to C and wrap 1in/2.5cm cuffs, starting at the wrists. Anchor and snip. Attach and wrap a piece of gold braid yarn around the neck to create the collar. Anchor and snip.

Skirt: Cut 40 pieces of B and eight pieces of C, each 12in/30.5cm long. Cut a 40in/102cm piece of B and fold it in half. Anchor it to a board and use it as a foundation for a lark's head knot fringe, each knot made up of two pieces of yarn. Make the fringe in this sequence: seven knots of B, two knots of C, six knots of B, two knots of C, seven knots of B. Trim the skirt evenly and tie it around the waist.

Belt: Cut a 50in/127cm piece each of gold yarn and gold floss. Hold the yarns together, and anchor the ends to a table or doorknob. Twist the yarns until they double back upon themselves. Wrap the rope just created around the waist two times, then knot the pieces together at the waist. Cut the tails so they are even in length, and knot the ends of each tail.

Hair: Wrap D 120 times around a 9in/23cm board. Follow the basic instructions for the hair. Sew hair to the head and trim evenly. Braid the front pieces of the hair on each side using six pieces of yarn, and one piece of gold floss tied onto the top of the braid. Tie the two braids together in a ponytail at the back of the head, using a 12in/30.5cm piece of gold floss.

Face: Follow the basic instructions for the Large Doll, using green floss to embroider the colored part of the eye.

From the Persian tale The Thousand and One Nights

FINISHED HEIGHT 11in/28cm

MATERIALS

Yarn

* Deborah Norville Collection™ Everyday® Soft Worsted 4oz/113g, approx. 203yds/186m (100% anti-pilling acrylic)—one skein each: #ED 100-35 Cappuccino (MC), #ED100-39 Bright Violet (A), #100-20 Orchid (B), C#100-32 Peony (C)

* Premier Yarns® Serenity® Sock Solids 1.76 oz/50g, approx. 230yds/210m (50% wool, 25% nylon, 25% rayon)—one skein each: #DN150-06 Deep Brown (D)

* Premier Yarns® Starry Night 1.75oz/50g, approx. 60yds/55m (90% nylon, 10% metallic)—one ball each: #3707 Majesty (E)

* Premier Yarns® Enchant® .88 oz/25g, approx. 429yds/393m (76% metallic, 24% payette)—one ball each: #29-02 Spun Gold (F)

Other Tools

* Sharp scissors, a ruler, stiff cardboard, and a large, blunt-tipped tapestry needle.

* Six-strand embroidery floss in black, white, brown, and rose pink

* Powder blush or paint for cheeks

* Pigma #01 micron marker in brown

DOLL

Follow the basic directions for the Large Doll using MC.

Shoes: Use A.

Pants/Bloomers: Wrap legs with MC. Use B to make the pants by wrapping the legs and hips. Start wrapping 1/8in/.3cm above the shoes.

Upper Body Color/Bandeau Shrug: Work upper body in MC. Make the bandeau by wrapping C around the upper chest 15 times. Anchor and snip. Cut a piece of C, 12in/30.5cm long, Fold the piece in half and insert it under the center front of bandeau, making sure the yarn tails are even. Bring the ends of the yarn through the fold to secure. Wrap the yarn a few times around the center of the bandeau, gathering it slightly. Tie the yarn tails together behind the neck. Trim the ends. Create the shrug by wrapping A around the right arm, behind the back, around the left arm, behind the back, repeating this pattern until the shrug is pleasing in appearance. Anchor and snip.

Skirt: Wrap E 33 times around a 5in/12.5cm board. DO NOT CUT THE FRINGE AT THE BOTTOM. Remove the yarn carefully from the board so the loops stay intact. Cut a 36in/91cm piece of B and fold it in half. Anchor it to a board and use it as a foundation for a lark's head knot fringe with 11 knots of three pieces of yarn each. Tie the skirt carefully around the waist. Wrap F around waist of the skirt until the knots are hidden. Anchor and snip.

Hair: Wrap D 160 times around a 9in/23cm board, and make hair following the basic directions. Cut a piece of F and tie around the head for a headband.

Face: Follow the basic directions for the Large Doll, using brown floss to embroider the colored part of the eye.

King Arthur

From the legend of King Arthur

FINISHED HEIGHT 11in/28cm

MATERIALS

Yarn

* Lion Brand® Yarns Vanna's Choice®
3.5oz/100g, 170yds/156m (100% acrylic):
one skein each: #860-098 Fisherman (MC),
#860-153 Black (A), # 860-149 Silver Grey (B),
#860-151 Charcoal Grey (C), and #860-130
Honey (D)

* Lion Brand® Yarns Vanna's Glamour®
1.75oz/50g, 202yds/185m (96% acrylic, 4%
other fiber)—one skein each: #861-171 Gold
(E), #861-186 Bronze (F)

* Lion Brand® Yarns Glitterspun®, approx.
16ft/5m (80% polyester, 20% nylon)—one
card each: #605-170 Gold (G), #605-150
Silver (H)

Other Tools

* Sharp scissors, a ruler, stiff cardboard, and a
large, blunt-tipped tapestry needle

* Six-strand embroidery floss in black, white,
green, and rose pink

* Powder blush or paint for cheeks

* Pigma #01 micron marker in brown

DOLL

Follow the basic directions for the Large Doll using
MC. Do not wrap the arms and legs with MC.

Boots/Legs: Use A for the shoes following the
basic directions for the Large Doll. Cover the legs
with B.

Shirt/Bloomers: Cover the arms with B. Cover the
body and make the bloomers with F. Note that
because you are using a fine yarn, you will have to
repeat the wrapping sequence a number of times
to cover. Wrap around each shoulder for 1in/2.5cm
using C, building up layers until the shoulders look
full.

Tunic Panels: Cut 20 pieces of D, 5in/12.5cm long.
Cut a 24in/61cm piece of D and fold it in half.
Anchor it to a board and use it as a foundation for a
lark's head knot fringe. There are five panels made
of two lark's head knots, each using two pieces of
yarn. There is a space between each panel. Trim the
ends to 2in/5cm. Tie the fringe around the waist.

Face: Follow the basic directions for the Large Doll,
using green floss to embroider the colored part of
the eye.

Hair: Following the basic directions for the hair,
wrap D 120 times over a 7in/18cm board. Trim hair
to shoulder length.

Crown: Cut four 60in/152cm pieces of E. Holding
all four strands together, attach them to a table or
doorknob. Twist the yarn until it doubles back upon
itself. Cut the rope just made from the anchored
end, and knot the end to secure. Tie the rope into a
crown that fits on the figure's head. Trim the ends.

Sword: For the hilt, wrap B around three fingers
ten times and tie at each end to make a bundle.
Put aside. Wrap C three times around a 7in/18cm
board. Tie with a knot at one end. This is the tip
of the sword. Wrap the opposite end of the sword
with H, for 1¾in/4.5cm to form a loop at the top of
the handle. Wrap yarn around the bottom of the
wraps, forming the circle handle at the top of the
sword. Place the hilt under the handle, and tie a
knot with a piece of yarn to hold the hilt in place.
Wrap the hilt with G, until the bundle is covered
and the hilt has a triangular shape. Anchor and
snip. Wrap H in a crisscross fashion around the bottom of the circle handle and around the hilt until
the coverage is pleasing, then wrap from the hilt to
the tip of the sword, building layers at the top of
the sword, until the sword has a triangular shape.
Anchor and snip.

Queen Guinevere

From the legend of King Arthur

FINISHED HEIGHT 11in/28cm (without crown)

MATERIALS

Yarn

* Lion Brand® Yarns Vanna's Choice® 3.5oz/100g, 170yds/156m (100% acrylic)— one skein each: #860-098 Fisherman (MC), #860-153 Black (A), #860-108 Dusty Blue (B), #860-124 Toffee (C), and #860-135 Rust (D)

* Martha Stewart Crafts™/MC Glitter Ribbon 1.75 oz/50g, approx. 69yds/63m (62% polyester, 38% metallic polyester)— one ball each: #5900-506 Blue Sapphire (E)

Other Tools

* Sharp scissors, a ruler, stiff cardboard, and a large, blunt-tipped tapestry needle

* Six-strand embroidery floss in black, dark aqua, white, and rose pink

* Powder blush or paint for cheeks

* Pigma #01 micron marker in brown

DOLL

Follow the basic directions for the Large Doll using MC. Do not wrap the legs with MC.

Shoes: Use A.

Legs/Bloomers: Use B.

Bodice/Upper Body Color: Wrap bodice using B, then wrap the arms about two thirds of the way from the shoulder to the wrist. Wrap E around the shoulders for 1in/2.5cm, building up layers at the shoulder to create a puffed sleeve. Anchor and snip. Repeat for other sleeve. Thread a tapestry needle with a 12in/30.5cm piece of A. Anchor it to the body and stitch two "X"s on the front of bodice to imitate lacing. Anchor and snip.

Skirt Wrap: Cut 4 pieces of A, 48 pieces of B, and 12 pieces of E, each 12in/30.5cm long. Cut a

24in/61cm piece of B and fold it in half. Anchor it to a board and use it as a foundation for a lark's head knot fringe. The sequence is 12 knots (two strands each) of B, 1 knot (two strands) of A, 5 knots (one strand each) of E, 1 knot (two strands) of A, and 12 knots (two strands each) of B. Trim the fringe evenly and tie it around the waist.

Face: Follow the basic instructions for the Large Doll, using dark aqua floss to embroider the colored part of the eye.

Hair: Follow the basic instructions for the Large Doll, using one strand each of C and D held together and wrapped 60 times. Once the hair is secured to the head and trimmed, make a braid on either side of the face using 12 strands of yarn.

Crown: Working from the skein, make a thick loop by wrapping B 30 times around three fingers. Cut the yarn from the skein, but leave the loop on the fingers. Cut a piece of B, 72in/183cm long. Tie it onto the loop, and cover the loop evenly by wrapping the yarn all the way around the loop. Knot at the end to secure. Remove it carefully from the fingers. Cut a 30/76cm piece of E. Leaving a tail of approx. 9in/23cm hanging, wrap the yarn around the crown, leaving the extra yarn hanging on each side. Affix the crown to the hair by pulling a clump of hair through the hole in the center of the crown.

Snowman

From "The Snow Man" by Hans Christian Andersen

FINISHED HEIGHT 10in/25cm

MATERIALS

Yarn

* Lion Brand® Vanna's Choice® 3.5oz/100g, 170yds/156m (100% acrylic)—one skein each: #860-100 White (MC), #860-100 Black (A), #860-124 Toffee (B)

* Lion Brand® Heartland® 5oz/142g, 251yds/230m (94% acrylic, 6% rayon)—one skein each: #136-171 Cuyahoga Valley (C), #136-105 Glacier Bay (D)

* Small amounts of orange yarn

Other Tools

* Sharp scissors, a ruler, stiff cardboard, and a large, blunt-tipped tapestry needle

* Six-strand embroidery floss in black

* Crochet hook (This will make it easier to form the knots for the hat.)

DOLL

Head and Body Bundle: Wrap MC 130 times around a 12in/30.5cm board. Tie with a constrictor knot (using MC) at each end of the bundle. Carefully remove from the board, placing a piece of paper between the front and back wraps to keep them separate. Wind a ball of yarn* 9½in/24cm in circumference to fill the head. Place it inside the bundle at the top edge. Using a piece of MC, tie a constrictor knot at the neck to form the head. Wind a ball of yarn* 12in/30.5cm in circumference to fill the body. Place it inside the body and set aside. The arms and legs will be placed in the same area.

*Use scrap yarn to wind the center of the balls of yarn that are used to fill the figures. Then wind an outer layer of the color needed. This will conserve yarn.

Arms: Wrap D 25 times around a 9in/23cm board. Make the hands following the directions for the Large Doll, using five strands for the thumbs. Cover the arms with B. Make mitten cuffs by wrapping around the wrists for 1in/2.5cm. Build up layers at the cuffs. Place the arms inside the body, above the ball in the body, and push them up, as close as possible to the head. Using MC, tie a constrictor knot under the arm bundle. The knot will be hidden by the scarf.

Legs: Wrap MC 55 times around a 9in/23cm board. Make the shoes using A and following the basic directions for the Large Doll. Wrap the legs with MC. Make boots by wrapping A for 1¾in/4.5cm from the ankles, building layers to create the appearance of a boot. Place the leg bundle inside the body, just below the ball filling the body. It will be a tight squeeze.

Hat: Cut 108 pieces each of C and D, 12in/30.5cm long. Make a series of lark's head knots, each with three strands of yarn all the way around the hairline, alternating knots of C and D. Using a piece of C, tie all of the pieces together with a constrictor knot, forming a pompom at the top of the hat. Trim the pompom. Using C from the skein, wrap around the hairline, for 1½in/4cm, covering the lark's head knots. Build up layers of wraps so that the wraps form the cuff of the hat. Anchor and snip.

Scarf: Cut 21 pieces each of C and D, 24in/61cm long. Make a three-section braid using 14 strands of mixed colors in each section of the braid. Tie with a piece of C about 1½in/4cm from each end to secure the braid.

Face: Thread a tapestry needle with four six-strand pieces of black embroidery floss; make colonial-knot eyes. Cut a 32in/81cm piece of orange yarn and wrap it around two fingers. Make a constrictor knot at the top of the wrapped yarn with a 60in/152cm piece of orange yarn. Carefully remove the bundle from your fingers. Wrap the yarn tails firmly around the bundle until it is covered evenly. Continue to wrap, building up layers until the nose takes on a triangular form. Anchor and snip one tail, securing the work. Use the other tail to sew the nose to the face. Anchor and snip all loose ends of floss to secure and hide.

Princess Trembling

From the Celtic tale "Fair, Brown and Trembling"

FINISHED HEIGHT 12in/30.5cm

MATERIALS

Yarn

* Red Heart® Super Saver™ 7oz/198g, approx. 364yds/333m (100% acrylic)—one skein each: #E300-313 Aran (MC), #E300-373 Petal Pink (A), #E300-368 Paddy Green (B)

* Red Heart® Soft® 5oz/141g, approx. 256yds/234m (100% acrylic)—one skein each: #E728-4422 Tangerine (C)

* Red Heart® Boutique Sashay Boho™ 3.5oz/100g, approx. 23 yds/21m (69% acrylic, 31% polyester)—one skein each: #E782B1967 Envy (D)

Other Tools

* Sharp scissors, a ruler, stiff cardboard, and a large, blunt-tipped tapestry needle

* Six-strand embroidery floss in black, white, dark aqua, and rose pink

* Powder blush or paint for cheeks

* Pigma #01 micron marker in brown

DOLL

Follow the basic directions for the Large Doll using MC.

Shoes: Use A.

Shirt/Bloomers: Wrap with A.

Skirt: Cut one piece of D 3 yds/2.75m long. Thread tapestry needle with an 18in/46cm piece of A and knot the end. Gather D yarn by running needle in and out of "ladder" at top edge of ruffle/tape yarn. Smooth gathers to make them even, then tie skirt around waist of doll. Anchor and snip.

Hair: Follow the basic directions for the Large Doll, using C. Make 16in/41cm braid from nine strands of A, using three strands in each section. Tie the braid around the hair to make a headband.

Face: Follow the basic directions for the Large Doll, using dark aqua floss to embroider the colored part of the eye.

Nisse

From Norwegian folklore

FINISHED HEIGHT 11½in/29cm from the feet to the tip of the hat

MATERIALS

Yarn

* Deborah Norville Collection™ Every-day® Soft Worsted 4oz/113g, approx. 203yds/186m (100% anti-pilling acrylic)—one skein each: #ED100-02 Cream (MC), #ED100-16 Kiwi (A), #100-01 Snow White (B), #100-7 Really Red (C)

* Premier® Yarns Wool Worsted 3.5oz/100g, approx. 186yds/170m (100% wool)—one skein each: #0121 Charcoal (D)

* Premier® Yarns Parfait™ 3.5/100g, approx. 192 yds/175m (100% polyester)—one skein each: #3002 Toffee (E)

Other Tools

* Sharp scissors, a ruler, stiff cardboard, and a large, blunt-tipped tapestry needle

* Six-strand embroidery floss in black, white, and rose pink

* Powder blush or paint for cheeks

* Pigma #01 micron marker in brown

* Crochet hook (This will make it easier to form the knots for the hair.)

DOLL

Follow the basic directions for the Large Doll using MC. Head/body/leg bundles are made with 50 wraps around a 9in/23cm board. Do not wrap the legs with MC. Fill the head with a ball that is 6in/15cm in diameter.

Boots/Legs/Bloomers: Make the shoes using E. Wrap legs and hips with D. Wrap in layers from the ankle up for ½in/1.25cm with E to make the boot tops. Anchor and snip.

Arms: Follow the basic directions for the Large Doll using C. The arm bundle is made with 35 wraps around a 7in/18cm board. Use five strands for the thumbs. Wrap the arms with A. Wrap the sleeves with a band of B to decorate.

Shirt: Wrap shirt with A. Wrap around hips to cover and create a tunic effect. Wrap a piece of C at lower waist for a decoration. Thread a tapestry needle with one piece of B, and stitch a straight-stitch star on front of the shirt. Anchor and snip.

Hair: Cut 48 pieces of B, each 7in/18cm long. Make a series of lark's head knots, each with two strands of yarn, all the way around the lower edge of the hairline. Use the tip of a needle to separate the strands of yarn. Trim the hair.

Hat: Cut 48 pieces of C, each 9in/23cm long. Make a series of lark's head knots, each with two strands of yarn, all the way around the hairline, directly inside the circle of hair knots. Using a piece of C, tie all the pieces of C together with a constrictor knot 1in/2.5cm from the top. This will form the pompom at the top of the hat. Trim the pompom. Make a small ball of C to fill the hat so it stands upright. Using C from the skein, wrap around the hairline, covering the lark's head knots for 1½in/4cm. Build up layers of wraps, so that the wraps form the cuff of the hat. Anchor and snip.

Face: Follow the basic directions for the Large Doll. Embroider pupils only for the eyes.

Scarf: Cut 12 pieces of D, each 12in/30.5cm long. Make a three-section braid using four strands of yarn in each section. Tie the braid with a piece of D at each end about 1½in/4cm from the bottom to secure.

Mermaid

From "The Little Mermaid" by Hans Christian Andersen

FINISHED HEIGHT 12in/30.5cm

MATERIALS

Yarn

* Premier® Yarns Deborah Norville Collection™ Everyday® Soft Worsted 4oz/113g, approx. 203yds/186m (100% acrylic)—one skein each: #1002 cream (MC), #1016 Kiwi (A)

* Premier® Yarns Deborah Norville Collection™ Everyday® Soft Worsted 3.5oz/100g, approx.180yds/165m (100% acrylic)—one skein each: #2021 Happy Baby (B)

* Premier® Yarns Spangle™, 1.76oz/50g, approx. 164yds/150m (75% nylon, 25% metallic)—one ball each: #0212 Caribbean Sparkle (C)

* Premier® Yarns Ever Soft® 3oz/80g, approx. 158yds/144.5m (100% acrylic)—one skein each: #0030 Tan (D)

Other Tools

* Sharp scissors, a ruler, stiff cardboard, and a large, blunt-tipped tapestry needle

* Six-strand embroidery floss in black, white, green, and rose pink

* Powder blush or paint for cheeks

* Pigma #01 micron marker in brown

* Crochet hook (This will make it easier to form the knots for the hair.)

DOLL

Follow the basic directions for the Large Doll, but do not make shoes.

Fin Piece: (Make 1) Using A, wrap the yarn 20 times around a 6in/15cm board. Tie the bundle firmly at each end with an 8in/20cm piece of A.

Head/Body/Tail: Make two head/body/leg bundles as in the basic directions for the Large Doll, using MC. Switch to A and knot a 4yd/3.7m piece of yarn to the middle of the bundle as if making

shoes. Wrap the yarn for 2in/5cm on each side of the center knot, making a 4in/10cm wrapped section. Fold this section in half at the center knot, forming a loop at bottom of each leg. Note that the opening for the loop should face the side of the doll, not the front, as with the basic shoe directions. Make the head and torso following the basic directions for the Large Doll. Using A from the skein, wrap each leg. Then build up the hips by wrapping a figure-8 pattern from the top of one leg to the top of the other leg 15 times, then wrap the yarn in a figure-8 pattern all the way down both legs, covering them evenly, down to the loops. Anchor and snip.

Make the head following the basic instructions.

Pinch one tied end of the fin piece and pull it through both tail loops at the bottom of the bundles, centering the fin carefully. Push the fin down to the bottom of the loops. Using A from the skein, wrap tightly from each knot end to the loops. Build up the yarn at the center; wrap forming a triangle shape, by alternating around the center piece, until pleasing in appearance. Wrap up from the fin to the hips.

Skirt: Cut 36 pieces each of B and C, 9in/23cm long. Cut an anchor of 30in/76cm piece of B and fold it in half. Anchor it to a board and use it as a foundation for a lark's head knot fringe of 18 knots, using one strand of each color held together. Wrap and tie the skirt around the waist. Trim the fringe so that it is uneven.

Bandeau Top: Using B, wrap yarn from the shoulders to the waist, eight times over each shoulder; repeat three times, layering and covering the chest. Anchor and snip. Wrap an 8in/20cm piece around the center front to create a bandeau effect.

Hair: Follow the basic instructions for hair, using D wrapped 120 times around a 9in/23cm board. Make three nine-strand braids on the left side of the head and two nine-strand braids on the right side of the face. Cut four 15in/38cm pieces of C and wrap them around the forehead, under some of the braids. Tie them behind the head for the headband.

Face: Follow the basic instructions for the Large Doll, using green floss to embroider the colored part of the eye.